Luther and the Peasants' War

Luther and the Peasants' War

LUTHER
AND
THE
PEASANTS' WAR

Luther's Actions and Reactions

Robert N. Crossley

An Exposition-University Book
EXPOSITION PRESS   NEW YORK

LIBRARY OF CONGRESS CATALOG CARD NUMBER: 73-92849
ISBN 0-682-47890-3

Manufactured in the United States of America

CONTENTS

ACKNOWLEDGMENTS

The present interest in ecumenism plus the 450th anniversary of the 95 Theses of Luther have increased the interest of many people in those stirring and remarkable events of the 16th century. Clergy and laymen alike have been forced to pay some attention to this dramatic and dynamic period in the history of civilization. Being one of the central figures Martin Luther has always been a prime subject for the historian, theologian, sociologist, philosopher, linguist and even the psychoanalyst. Many have asserted that more has been written about Luther than any other personality in the history of Western civilization. During the 450th anniversary of his famous Theses, this material has been added to by special lectures, convocations, sermons from the pulpits, symposia, etc. This interest by Protestant, Roman Catholic, and non-Christian scholars is not only natural but understandable. The movement begun by Luther was and is important not only for Europe or even confined to the Western world. It has world importance, and this continues to the present day.

To the student of Luther and the Early Reformation there are many problems and obstacles which must be faced. Not the least of these is the superabundance of material which has been published and undoubtedly will continue to be published. No single individual can possibly be acquainted with this mass of material. The secular historian will overlook much that interests the theologian. The theologian will do likewise.

Added to the mass of material available there are also the biases and prejudices of both the writer and the reader. These too are legion. Such bias and prejudice will not be absent from this present work. The reader has to be aware of them and beware.

I owe much gratitude to many, many people. I wish to thank Professor Albert Hyma for his interest and enthusiasm during those student days, when as a graduate student I was first introduced by Professor Hyma to Luther research. I wish, too, to thank St. Olaf College for the opportunity to be relieved of teaching and other duties so that this book could be completed, and the University of Michigan which granted me that remarkable title, *Visiting Scholar,* which allowed me the use of the facilities of the University during that sabbatical year.

To the library personnel of both St. Olaf College and the University of Michigan a special thanks is necessary. Without their help and kindness conditions would have been far more difficult than they were.

Without the encouragement and assistance of my wife this work could never have been completed.

Although encouragement, interest and assistance have been received, and gratefully so, any errors in the present work are mine and mine alone. And I take and accept full responsibility for those conclusions and judgments even though these might differ from those of the reader.

INTRODUCTION

Luther's appearance before the Diet of Worms in the spring of 1521 is a definite dividing line in the life and career of the reformer. Up until that dramatic appearance Luther was an individual known only in the Germanies. Until the posting of the 95 Theses in 1517 he wasn't even that. Until 1517 he had only a very limited reputation, limited to certain university circles in Saxony and to parts of western Germany. Between 1517 and 1521 that reputation was expanded. The events at Worms gave to Luther a reputation among all of the states of the Empire as Alexander rightly reported to Rome. By 1530 Luther's name was known throughout practically all of western and central Europe.

Luther's life had already been filled with drama and with dramatic events. The years in the monastery, the trip to Rome, the controversy brought about by the indulgence matter, the struggles within the University of Wittenberg, his revolutionary discoveries of Justification by Faith and the Priesthood of All Believers all have provided rewarding material for the biographer, the writer of monographic studies, and the researcher in many different fields. And the researcher, whatever his field, has an abundance of material which is staggering. The drama and polemics did not end at Worms. In a sense Worms was another beginning.

One of the most disturbing and perhaps one of the most interesting events of the early Reformation was the Peasants' War, 1524-1525. Peasant uprisings and rebellions were certainly not unknown in European history. The late Middle Ages and Renaissance periods witnessed many of the examples of discontent and unrest among the peasants of Europe. But the war of 1524-1525 was far greater in extent and in numbers involved. Furthermore, the events in the 16th century had the stimulus and the influence of the early Reformation as an added factor. Although earlier uprisings might well have had religion as one of the elements or ingredients, the 16th century war saw religion as one of the major factors. Also the prime mover of the Reformation, Martin Luther, was intimately involved. This last ingredient makes the war of special importance to the student of the Reformation and the Reformation Era.

The present study is an effort to examine Luther and Luther's actions and reactions during that war. The war was a serious test of Luther and his leadership; it was also a test of the reform movement which he led. Luther has been charged with being antipeasant. He has been called a tool of the princes. He has been accused of fomenting rebellion; that his revolt against the church gave a reason for the peasant class to rebel against their lords and masters. He has been condemned for his violent and intemperate language as found in his tracts written on the peasant uprising. He has been condemned and criticized for his marriage in the very midst of the revolt. The criticisms and condemnations of Luther have been legion. And much of this centers around his actions and reactions during the war of 1524-1525.

This present work has concentrated on Luther's political and economic status and ideas in order to explain or partially explain why Luther acted as he did. As the leader of the reform movement in Saxony, and as a parish pastor, Luther was forced by circumstances to write and sermonize on many subjects. He wrote on politics and he wrote on economic matters. By studying Luther's tracts, sermons, and letters, a great deal can be gleaned about his economic and political ideas. Much of the printed matter comes from the period prior to 1525 so its timing is especially helpful to the student interested in the revolt and in this stage of the Reformation.

To the person interested in historiography, the Peasants' War also is of tremendous interest. It is one of those events in history which demonstrate so well the influence and pressure of current events and the contemporary scene on the writing of history. Not only has attention been given to Luther's position during the war, but other topics have also come to the fore. Münzer's role in that war and Münzer's role in the Reformation have been the concern of a large number of scholars, some of them Communists, who have discovered Münzer to be the folk hero and leader of the "People's Reformation." The war has also caused considerable concern among the present heirs of 16th-century Anabaptism. Were those leaders of the peasants in 1524 and 1525 related to 16th-century Anabaptism? Was the war another example of the radicalism which Münzer in the 1520's was to show? Present writers are demonstrating that the leaders of the peasants were not Anabaptists, at least as they define them. The war has also brought out considerable publication of documentary material relating to the war itself. Source books are now available for the student of the early 16th century. Interest in the war and the Reformation have also resulted in reprints of earlier works which have long been out of print. Bax's work is an example of this. Textbook publishers have also gotten into the act since one of the problem series in European history concentrates on the Peasants' War.

Yet for all of the interest on various other subjects and topics related to the War, Martin Luther remains the primary subject, hence this present study. But this present study goes beyond Luther's actions and reactions during the war, as important as these topics are. This work also studies two other critical events which were also tests of Luther's leadership and tests of the movement which he headed: namely, the Wittenberg Disturbances, 1521-1522 and the Knights' Revolt, 1522-1523. These two problems were examined to discover Luther's actions and reactions in an earlier period when his church was threatened or so he thought. They were also examined to discover if Luther was consistent or whether he changed his mind on political matters and economic affairs. Did he vacillate? Did he write only under the impact of the immediate problems or did he take a position which he held for some time? There is no attempt to show any connection between the Peasants' War and the earlier rebellions.

The attempt has been made to study Luther's ideas and actions in the early 1520's and compare and contrast them with his actions and ideas during the war.

The entire decade of the 1520's was of critical importance to Luther. In fact, this decade might be entitled the critical years or the testing years.

1.

THE WITTENBERG DISTURBANCES

On the night of 25 April 1521, Martin Luther made preparations to leave the city of Worms. It had been a trying time for the German monk. He had been called upon to defend his writings and his position before an august body of clergy and imperial nobles including the young emperor, Charles V. He had stated his position as clearly as possible. He could do no more. It was now necessary for him to return to his position on the faculty at the University of Wittenberg and to resume his teaching and public ministry. However, Luther was not to see Wittenberg for over six months. Although the Edict of Worms was not published until late May, 1521, Luther's supporters and followers deemed it necessary that precautions be taken to secure the life of their famous leader who stood condemned as an heretic and branded an outlaw before Worms. On the night of 25 April 1521, Luther was informed by his friend, Georg Spalatin, that on the way to Wittenberg, his party would be taken by surprise and captured.[1] Only a few people were to know of the plot. Luther himself was made aware of his destination, the famous Wartburg Castle. But Nicholas Amsdorf, who was to accompany Luther, did not know the ultimate destination of his friend. Shortly after his arrival at the castle Luther wrote to Spalatin on 14 May 1521, "Amsdorf knew of course that I was to be captured by somebody, but did not know the place of my captivity."[2]

On 26 April 1521, the small party left Worms. After a rather leisurely journey, during which the party was surprised and Luther captured, the famous monk arrived at the Wartburg castle on 3 May 1521. He was immediately secluded in a small room as far removed as possible from the castle's retainers. During the first few weeks the German Augustinian monk was transformed outwardly in appearance to a German knight and noble, the

Junker Georg. It was at this time that Luther allowed his hair and beard to grow in order to defy detection and recognition. But appearances were not enough. The monk also had to learn something about the way of life of a 16th-century knight, and so he received instructions in the arts and manners of knighthood. The secrecy concerning Luther's whereabouts was remarkable. Only a few close friends knew where he was. Fortunately, rumors were widely circulated that he had fled Saxony, and rumors even indicated that he had fled the Germanies. The confusion resulting from this aided in protecting Luther. It is not known for how long Luther had intended to stay at the Wartburg. Certainly he did not relish the idea of remaining in hiding for too long a time. In fact, he was anxious to return to Wittenberg; but he had accepted the advice of Spalatin that it would be to his advantage, and to the advantage of the Elector of Saxony, if he were kept in safe hiding until it could be ascertained what the authorities would do concerning the Edict of Worms. However, he had made a reservation. He intended to return to Wittenberg sometime around Easter, 1522.[3] During his sojourn at the Wartburg, meanwhile, he could accomplish a great deal of work. After that date, he would have to return and resume his public teaching and ministry.

If Luther had returned directly to Wittenberg, assuming of course that he would have been safe, he and his city might not have been plagued by the disturbances which so upset him when he began to receive reports of the situation there. A strong hand was needed at Wittenberg at this time. The movement that was being inaugurated by Luther needed Luther himself to direct it, not his followers and associates. This became quite apparent during his absence. While he was at the Wartburg, the leadership in Wittenberg fell to three men: Philip Melanchthon, professor of Greek and Luther's closest associate and dearest friend; Karlstadt, professor of theology and archdeacon at the Castle Church; and Gabriel Zwilling, a monk of Luther's own order. Events were to prove that Melanchthon was neither the administrator, organizer, nor strong personal leader that was so necessary at this time. He was too easily influenced by others, particularly by Karlstadt,

Zwilling, and the Zwickau Prophets who came to Wittenberg early in 1522. Luther's earlier tracts, "An Address to the German Nobility" and the "Babylonian Captivity of the Church," were causing widespread discussions and were influencing people more than the author suspected in 1521 and early 1522, when he was absent and could not personally direct the movement they had engendered. Wittenberg provides an excellent example of what the writings and teachings of Luther could do when he was not present to direct affairs. When he was absent the movement was apt to become more radical than he desired.

During Luther's stay at the Wartburg, the Reformation which he had begun did not stop; nor did it slow down. On the contrary, under the proddings of Karlstadt and Zwilling, the movement actually gained momentum. Much that Luther had advocated in previous tracts was adopted; much also was inaugurated that Luther did not specifically mention but which seemed to be implied in his writings and public pronouncements. Under the influence of Karlstadt and Zwilling, steps were taken at Wittenberg which later aroused the ire of Luther and brought his condemnation of these two men. As archdeacon of the Castle Church, Karlstadt held a commanding and influential position. From this pulpit this professor of theology at the University of Wittenberg urged three important reforms:[4]

1. Mass was to be abolished.

2. Communion in both kinds was to be given to the laity.

3. Marriage was urged for the clergy: priests and monks alike. But this zealot did more than just preach and exhort the people from the pulpit. He introduced communion in both kinds to his congregation, actually forcing them to take the bread into their own hands. He preached that it was in fact a sin to receive only the bread.[5] He further urged that images were wrong and advocated their abolition. Organs were also condemned since Karlstadt considered that they belonged only to theatrical exhibitions and princes' palaces.[6] As a demonstration of the position of the clergy in this new movement, Karlstadt removed his priestly vestments and conducted services in the ordinary garb of the layman. Apparently, he did not go quite so far as the Augustinian monk

Zwilling, who conducted church services with a feather in his beret. This former monk must have presented quite a sight in gay clothes with a beret jauntily stuck on his head with a feather whirling in the breeze. Karlstadt also became an example for the other clergy with regard to marriage. He himself took as a bride a young girl of 15 years. He was acting as an example for all to follow, and was determined to practice what he preached. Other innovations occurring in Wittenberg during Luther's absence included using native German during portions of the church service, discontinuing masses for the dead, and permitting monks and nuns, even urging them, to leave their cloisters for the outside world. Under the urgings of Zwilling, Luther's own order in Wittenberg in January, 1522, allowed monks to go free if they wished.[7] Up to Christmas, 1521, the above innovations had been carried through rather peacefully and without incident. Undoubtedly, there were members of the congregation of the Castle Church who were horrified at the new service. Others, however, welcomed these innovations joyously. But as Zwilling and Karlstadt warmed to their task, their ideas were copied and expanded by others until gradual change was no longer the rule. It was rapid and irrevocable.

At the Wartburg Luther had received reports of the events in Wittenberg, and since there had been no violence to speak of (he was accustomed to occasional student pranks and considered any sporadic outbursts as inspired by them), he was fairly pleased with the situation. At least, he did not deem it necessary to return permanently at this time. However, he had written three important tracts which had not yet been published: *On the Abolition of Private Masses, On Monastic Vows,* and *A Blast Against the Archbishop of Mainz.* Since Luther was anxious for these to be circulated among the people, he decided to make a quick trip to Wittenberg to find out why they had not appeared. In early December, 1521, therefore, he left the Wartburg. He went secretly and continued his disguise as Junker Georg. It is significant that on this visit of 4 December 1521 Luther did nothing publicly to stem the tide of the revolutionary activity in

Wittenberg. The situation there did not become serious until after his return once more to the Wartburg.

Late December, 1521, and early January, 1522, were the times when the events in Wittenberg became extremely serious. On Christmas Eve 1521, both the parish and Castle Churches were scenes of wild disorder. Altars were destroyed and images were cast out of the churches. Although some 15 monks had left the Augustinian monastery as early as 30 November 1521, on 6 January 1522, the chapter in Wittenberg decreed that those wishing to leave might do so freely. On 11 January 1522, Gabriel Zwilling so inflamed his followers and the attending mob that the side altars of the old convent church were destroyed by the monks, and again images were cast out.

The situation in Wittenberg was further complicated by the arrival of the Zwickau Prophets in late December, 1521. Their arrival coincides with the increasing tempo of violence and property destruction not present when Luther had visited the city in early December. Of the three men who arrived on 27 December 1521 (Nicholas Storch, Thomas Drechsel, and Marcus Stübner) Storch and Stübner are particularly important because of their ideas and activities.

Storch who had been allied in Zwickau with Thomas Müntzer before Storch's flight from the city believed that God revealed his will to him through dreams and visions. He held conversations with angels and even with God Himself. He rejected original sin, infant baptism, and the authority of scripture. He preached vigorously against luxury and the vanities, and had a strong appeal to the lower classes with his call for the common ownership of all property.

Marcus Stübner had been a student at Wittenberg and was known to the members of the faculty. In December he accepted housing from Philip Melanchthon during his stay there.

Storch and Drechsel left Wittenberg shortly after, probably in early January, but Stübner remained for a longer period. Shortly after Luther's return in March, Luther had occasion to meet the prophets who had continued their wanderings. By September,

1522, he had had brief discussions with the three. Needless to say, he never agreed with their views, and he came to consider that their spirit was satanic. Whether he really understood them is of course questionable.[8]

Because of this wanton destruction of property which threatened to get out of hand, the Town Council of Wittenberg was forced to act. The members of the council were fearful that destruction of real estate would next be visited on the Town Church which was directly under the jurisdiction of the council. None of the other churches so far which had been the scene of riots and lootings were under the control of the council, and as such the council had no jurisdiction in those cases. However, the Town Church was another matter. In December, 1521, the council chamber had been invaded by a group of citizens who demanded of the three councillors present that they abolish the mass and institute communion in both kinds for all.[9] As a result of the pressure, direct and indirect, the Town Council met with faculty representatives from the University of Wittenberg and drafted and there adopted "The Worthy Ordinance for the Princely City of Wittenberg."[10]

Basically The Worthy Ordinance was a moderate and even a modest document. It was an attempt by the council to silence the more rabid radicals among the Wittenbergers. However, the ordinance was not successful in this aim since violence continued. The ordinance covered four main points:

1. The mass was to be conducted similarly to that of Karlstadt's service in the Castle Church. This was to include communion in both kinds for the laity. Parts of the service were to be conducted in German so all could understand, and the pastor was to be allowed to conduct divine service in street clothes if he wished.

2. Begging, a medieval curse, was forbidden within the city limits.

3. A common fund was to be established for the maintenance of the poor. This naturally supplemented point two, and it was hoped that a common fund would eliminate the need for begging. It is interesting to note that part of the common fund was

to be derived from the costly and beautiful cases where images and relics were displayed for public viewing.

4. All images were to be removed.

As we have seen, these were the basic aims of both Karlstadt and Zwilling in their preaching of reform. Naturally, the ordinance said nothing about marriage of the clergy. The Town Council felt that this was not within the province nor competency of the councillors to decide. Nor was the ordinance specific concerning music or the actual details of the church service. It was not a rigid document where the formalities or worship were set down and were for evermore to be followed without deviation. It was meant to be moderate as well as modest in its articles. It was hoped that it would placate the radicals to a certain extent, and at the same time not offend the more conservative elements within the city. Yet The Worthy Ordinance was a model for future cities. It was the first city ordinance of the Reformation, and as such an important document in the history of the Reformation. Significantly, perhaps, it was adopted without Luther, for the Reformer was not consulted about the provisions of the ordinance. At no time did Luther publicly attack the provisions of the ordinance, nor did he chide or criticize the members of the Town Council for adopting it. It must be noted, however, that many of the provisions were neglected by Luther when he did return and assumed control and direction once more of the reform movement. It is interesting to note, however, that Luther did become interested and involved in the idea of a common Chest. In 1523 he wrote a preface for "The Ordinance of a Common Chest."[11]

Luther had been very busy at the Wartburg, writing tracts, writing letters, and translating the New Testament into German. One of his major tasks was the composition of Postiles which form one of the best guides for studying Luther's development. However, he could not stay in the castle indefinitely. How long he considered remaining in hiding is not known. Apparently, he decided to leave around Easter, 1522, but his return was hastened by the events in Wittenberg. As was mentioned above, Luther had made a quick trip to the city in December, 1521, not because of disturbing reports about events there, but rather to find out why a number of recently written tracts had not yet appeared in print. After his December 4th visit, events proceeded more rapidly, and he became very annoyed with the radicals in the city. Already, in January, 1522, rumors of greater and more radical changes were being received by him. And these rumors greatly disturbed him, so much so that a return visit was not unlikely. In January, he wrote to Georg Spalatin, "Rumors are circulated to the effect that changes have been made in the sacrament of the Lord's Supper. I went to Wittenberg before, but now I daily hear of greater changes."[12] Shortly after his return to the city in March, 1522, he adequately summed up his reasons for returning in a letter to his friend Wenceslaus Link, on 19 March 1522:

"Satan invaded my sheepfold and caused the liberty of the spirit to be changed into the license of the flesh, and when the service of love had been lost, to confound everything by a dreadful schism. Karlstadt and Gabriel Zwilling were the originators of these monstrosities. This was the reason why I returned, so that I might, if Christ were willing, destroy this work of Satan."[13]

On 1 March 1522 Luther left the Wartburg for the return journey to his city of Wittenberg. No longer was he to be the Junker Georg hiding from his enemies. He was again to be Martin Luther, preacher, teacher, and leader. On the return trip he stopped in Borna on 5 March 1522, and from here he wrote his famous letter to the Elector of Saxony, Frederick the Wise: "I would have you know that I come to Wittenberg with a higher protection than that of Your Grace. I do not ask you to protect me. I will protect you more than you will protect me. If I thought you would protect me, I would not come. This is not a case for the sword but for God, and since you are weak in the faith you cannot protect me. You ask what you should do, and think you have done too little. I say you have done too much and you should do nothing but leave it to God. You are excused if I am captured or killed. As a prince you should obey the emperor and offer no resistance. No one should use force except the one who is ordained to use it. Otherwise there is rebellion against God. But I hope you will not act as my accuser. If you leave the door open, that is enough. If they try to make you do more than that, I will then tell you what to do. If Your Grace had eyes, you would see the glory of God."[14]

On Thursday 6 March 1522 Luther arrived in Wittenberg, and began to prepare the series of eight sermons which were to start on the first Sunday in Lent.[15] It was this series of eight sermons which had a tremendous effect on the people of Wittenberg. Here now before them was the leader of the reform movement in person. As a result of these sermons Wittenberg bowed to law and order. Karlstadt was silenced. Even before the sermons were finished, Gabriel Zwilling confessed that he had been wrong.[16] The city of Wittenberg led by the Town Council, gave Luther substantial gifts in recognition of his success in bringing an end to the disturbances and restoring law and order once more in the city.

On Sunday 6 March 1522 in the Parish Church, the same church where Karlstadt had so vehemently carried through the reform which had contributed to the disturbances, Luther gave the first and longest of the eight sermons.[17] In this first sermon he began by listing four chief concepts in Christianity:

1. We are all the children of wrath.
2. God has sent us His only-begotten son.
3. There must be love.
4. We need patience.

On the first two, Luther stated that nothing seemed to be lacking or amiss in respect to these. They had been rightly preached. When it came to love, this was something else. He said that he saw no sign of love among them. They had not been grateful to God for His rich gifts and treasury. Nor did he see any real patience among them. It was necessary to go slowly and especially to recognize and tolerate the weakness of one's brother. "I would not have gone so far as you have done, if I had been there. What you did was good, but you have gone too fast. For there are also brothers and sisters on the other side who belong to us, and must still be won."[18] He chastized the congregation for not only going too far and too fast, but also because the changes were not accomplished in an orderly way. For example, all had erred who had consented and helped to abolish the mass—in itself a good undertaking, if accomplished in an orderly and peaceful manner. But it was done in wantonness, with no regard to proper order and accomplished with offense to many. The people should have obtained the aid of the authorities. They should have gone to the city authorities and requested through orderly process that changes be made.

He also chastised his congregation for not seeking his counsel: "I was not so far away that you could not reach me with a letter, especially since I did not interfere with you in any way. Did you want to begin something, and then leave me to shoulder the responsibility? That is more than I can undertake, and I will not do it." After a discussion of the above, Luther then turned to a discussion of two words: Must and Free. It was necessary to decide where each is applicable. He admonished the congregation not to confuse the two. Do not mistake what is free for a must. Do not force a person to eat meat on Friday. The eating of flesh on any day is a matter of free choice, and forcing someone to eat meat is definitely wrong. In the second sermon of Monday 10 March, Luther continued the discussion of Must and Free. And he also took up the topics of the Private Mass and the use of Images. In both cases he stated quite frankly that he considered the private mass and the use of idols or images to be wrong. Yet no one should be forced to give them up. "It should be preached and taught with tongue and pen, that to hold mass in such a manner is a sin, but no one should be dragged away from it by force."[19] As for images he cited the example of St. Paul who on a visit to Athens had visited the temple of the Greeks and noticed there a profusion of idols. Yet he did not destroy them, but left the temple and went outside and there he preached to the people against the use of idols. Luther constantly maintained that it was wrong to use force to bring about reforms. He himself had never used force, and yet he had accomplished much. In fact, he had done more than the congregation when they used force. Force and coercion only resulted in trouble and could result in bloodshed and violence. He could have done just that, but it would have been wrong. "Had I desired to foment trouble, I could have brought great bloodshed upon Germany. Yea, I could have started such a little game at Worms that even the emperor would not have been safe. But what would it have been? A fool's play. I did nothing; I left it to the Word."[20]

In sermon three delivered on Tuesday 11 March 1522, Luther continued on the discussion of Free and Must. And here in a rather short sermon he made a short list of those things which are a matter of choice:

1. Marriage.
2. Eating of fish or flesh.
3. The Monastic life.
4. Use of Images.

In the fourth sermon of Wednesday 12 March, Luther amplified his thoughts on those mattters which are purely matters of choice to the individual and which cannot be thrust upon him. Even the use of images is a matter of choice although he himself stated that they should be abolished because they are abused. Yet if there were only one person who used images properly, they could not be abolished by force.

On Thursday 13 March Luther delivered the fifth and one of the most pointed sermons in the entire series. He had to discuss a rather delicate point. This was the communion or the sacrament of the Lord's supper. He knew that during the reforms in Wittenberg prior to his return the sacrament had been given in both kinds to the laity. He also knew that Karlstadt had even gone so far as to insist that the communicants take the bread in their own hands during the ceremony. In the reports which Luther had received of these goings-on he had been told how some of the congregation actually quaked with fear and in fact fainted at being forced to handle the body of the Lord. Other members seemed to be enjoying themselves in a rather lewd manner at having gained suddenly such freedom. In this sermon, "A Sermon on the Sacrament," Luther denounced the belief and practice that the communicant must handle the sacrament. He admitted that it was not a sin to touch the bread as many had done; yet it was not a good work because it caused offense to

many. Again he emphasized the lack of force for reform. It is
necessary and good that the sacrament be received in both kinds,
yet it should not be made compulsory. But Luther did have a
solution for those who felt it necessary to handle the sacrament
personally. "But if there is anyone so stupid that he must touch
the sacrament with his hands, let him have it brought to his
house and there let him handle it to his heart's content."[21] As
to how often a person should receive the sacrament, Luther made
no hard and fast rule. He denounced any law forcing one to receive the sacrament so many times a year. It depended on the
individual: his need and fitness to receive it. In fact, Luther
stated that today, Friday 14 March 1522, he was fit for the sacrament, but perhaps tomorrow he would not be fit or perhaps
he would have no need of it. "Yea, it may be that for six months
I have no desire nor fitness for it."[22] He also stated that one of
the fruits of the sacrament was Love. However, he had not per-
ceived that there was any love among the people in Wittenberg,
although there was much preaching of love, and certainly they
ought to practice it above all other things.

The last sermon of the series of eight was devoted to quieting the disturbances concerning confession. Here again Luther
showed his abhorrence of the use of force. Neither should confession be forbidden, nor should private confession be forced on
anyone.

The events at Wittenberg which had begun in December,
1521, and continued until the return of Luther in March, 1522,
were a severe and serious test of the new movement led by the
Wittenberg professor. It was not only a test of the ideas and
ideals of the movement; it was also an acid test of the leadership
of Luther himself. In many respects, he approved what had been
done at Wittenberg during his absence. He approved the abolition of images, the serving of the sacrament in both kinds to the
laity, the eating of meat on Friday, the marriage of clergy, and
so forth. These were good, and he did approve of them. But it
was the manner in which the reforms were carried through that
angered him. Again and again he preached that these reforms
could not come about by force. Only through the Word could

they be accomplished. He admitted that the images had been greatly abused by people. Many worshipped them, which was against God's commandments. Others gave images and relics to churches in hope of receiving grace from God as a good work. Both were absolutely wrong. And he admonished the princes and lords for lavishing such gifts on the various churches throughout the land.[23] Yet there might exist a few people who did not worship the images or who had donated them in hopes of receiving God's grace. Where would he, Luther, be if he forced the abolition of these things in respect to these few good people? What would his answer be to the devil who would certainly take him to task for depriving innocent and worthy people of the means of expressing their veneration of the Lord?

These reforms should be carried out peacefully and with due respect to law and order. As stated above, the people had had the opportunity of seeking Luther's counsel and advice concerning these matters even though he was absent from Wittenberg. The people also should have sought the aid of the city authorities before taking any action themselves.

Luther's actions upon his return from the Wartburg demonstrated two important facts:

1. The esteem and respect which Luther commanded among the congregation and people of Wittenberg.

2. His unwavering position concerning the manner of reform. He treated the congregation in attendance at the sermons as erring children. He cajoled and scolded, and was alternately firm and gentle in his speech to them. Yet there was never any doubt as to where he stood. The people had been wrong, terribly wrong. He was not going to shoulder the blame for what they had done. They could not do anything they pleased, and then expect him and his associates to take all the responsibility for their misdeeds. In these eight sermons he was able to stem the tide of radicalism at Wittenberg. The reform would continue to progress, but it would proceed in a very orderly and peaceful fashion. It is really remarkable that after the excesses of January and February, 1522, Luther was able once more to regain the leadership with absolutely no trouble. His actions in March,

1522, demonstrated beyond a doubt that he was the absolute
leader of the movement. Splinter groups might arise, but they
would not survive in Wittenberg. Nothing could or would be
done without his authorization and advice. He had quickly put
a stop to the excess and abuses which had occurred during his
absence. He was now once more in full command of the situation.

The events in Wittenberg during Luther's absence portended
the future. His first real exposure to the radicals whom he was
to call "Schwärmer" resulted in a victory, a victory at least in the
sense that the radical element in Wittenberg had been silenced.
But these radicals could not be silenced everywhere. Other radicals were to appear resulting in further disturbances elsewhere
at future times.

It is remarkable that Luther seemed unaware in 1522 just
what influence his writings were having in Europe. He seems
unaware that some of the tracts did lend themselves to interpretation and to broad implications. He seems to have refused
to accept such things.

The events of 1522 also demonstrate what could happen during Luther's absence. Perhaps it is unfortunate that the radical
elements (perhaps bound to arise in any case) arose when
Luther was in hiding away from the center of the reform movement in Saxony.

2.

THE KNIGHTS' REVOLT

The second of the great problems which faced Martin Luther
after his appearance before the Diet of Worms was the Knights'
Revolt in 1522 and 1523. The leaders of this revolt were the same
men, namely Franz von Sickingen and Ulrich von Hutten, who
had offered to protect and secure the person of the Augustinian

monk just before his appearance before Charles V. But these knights were no longer living in an age where the Free Knight of the Empire could exercise great political, military, and economic power. In fact, the position of the Free Knight was an anachronism. The knight was outmoded, obsolete; he was a person who had no place, politically, militarily, or economically in the empire of the 16th century.

Certainly warfare had changed enough to make the knight with his armor and small band of retainers obsolete. The use of mercenary armies raised by the territorial princes within the empire or by the kings in England and France had outmoded the knightly bands bound by oaths of fealty and homage. Moreover, the introduction of gunpowder made knights almost useless in warfare. The development of artillery had outclassed the great fortresses and castles which had been the haven and refuge of the knightly class. The Hundred Years' War between England and France had demonstrated that feudal chivalry as represented by the knights was a thing of the past.

Nevertheless the Free Knight did enjoy a peculiar position within the Empire. The Imperial Free Knight was classed as an Immediate Member of the Empire. He enjoyed immediacy (*Reichsunmittelbarkeit*). No lord stood between him and the emperor. He was a free lord of the empire (*reichsfreie Herr*). Although he was classed as immediate, nevertheless he did not have a vote in the imperial diet, and as a result his group was not considered to be an estate of the empire. Only estates of the empire (*Reichsstände*) could vote in the imperial diets. A class similar to the imperial knights were the imperial villages which were also immediate, but did not vote in the diet, and thus were not estates. This position of having immediacy but not being classed as estates demonstrates their peculiar position, at least politically.

Many of these knights looked back to the good old days when they were the real power in the land or when they held the balance of power between two great rival lords. Or they looked back to the days when they could exact tolls across fords or through passes and could collect such tolls even by using force if neces-

sary. In an age now where manufacturing and commerce were
playing increasingly important roles, and where it was in the
interest of the great princes to foster commerce and banking, the
knight and the knightly class were outmoded. He retained his
privileges at least politically, but economically and militarily he
was only a vestige of the long dead past. Preserved Smith in his
Age of the Reformation gives a good description of the declining
importance of the knightly class:

"This class, now in a state of moral and economic decay, had
long survived any usefulness it had ever had. The rise of the
cities, the aggrandizement of the princes, and the change to a
commercial from a feudal society all worked to the disadvantage
of the smaller nobility and gentry. About the only means of livelihood left them was freebooting, and that was adopted without
scruple and without shame. Envious of the wealthy cities, jealous
of the greater princes and proud of their tenure immediately from
the emperor, the knights longed for a new Germany, more cen-
tralized, more national, and of course, under their special direction."[1]

In 1522 two men, representing the knightly class, made one
last serious attempt to regain their lost position in the face of
almost insurmountable odds. These two men were Ulrich von
Hutten and Franz von Sickingen.[2] Hutten's family belonged to
the ranks of the nobility. At the tender age of eleven years little
Ulrich was placed in the convent at Fulda where he was to be
educated, and possibly to receive the training requisite for the
clergy. Perhaps his parents hoped that he would bring honor
and prestige to the name of Hutten as had Ulrich's cousin, Moritz,
who at 36 years of age had become the Bishop of Eichstatt. However, before Ulrich took any vows, he fled the convent. It is significant that in later years one can find no hint of bitterness or
regret in Hutten's speech or writings concerning his stay at Fulda.
On the contrary, he always spoke with respect of the cloister at
Fulda. But he had come to realize that he was not suited to becoming a monk, and thus had fled. With the flight from the

cloister in 1505, Hutten began the career of the goliard, the itinerant, mendicant scholar of the Middle Ages. As was common, he shifted from one university to another. During this period of his wanderings Hutten at times was reduced to abject poverty. He was forced to become in effect a human parasite, sponging off his friends at every turn. He had entered the University of Erfurt, but soon moved to the University at Frankfort-on-the-Oder. In 1506 he received the Bachelor of Arts degree at Frankfort. It was during his student days that the young nobleman experienced a shift in his own thinking, from scholasticism to humanism.[3] After Frankfort he went south to Vienna, but his arrogant bearing made his tenure in Vienna impossible. In April, 1512, he was at Pavia in the Italian peninsula, and he became so destitute that he was forced to take military service as a means of securing a living. In 1513 he was once more back in Germany.

During these years of wandering, Ulrich von Hutten, through his writings, had acquired a considerable reputation as a scholar and as a humanist. He was to put these literary talents to work for his family and for what he also believed to be for the cause of Germany. He first was to defend the honor and reputation of the Hutten name. The Hutten clan was determined to avenge a monstrous wrong which had been done to one of its members. Duke Ulrich of Württemberg had murdered a Hans von Hutten. The murder was supposedly caused by the Duke's admiration for Hans' wife. Ulrich undertook to use his considerable literary ability to inflame public opinion against the wicked duke. By March, 1519, he once more exchanged the pen for the sword. The Swabian League's forces with both Hutten and Sickingen in attendance were able to defeat Duke Ulrich of Württemberg. During the preparations for the campaign against Württemberg, Hutten became better acquainted with Franz von Sickingen. In fact, they shared the same tent during the campaign.

At this time Sickingen was at the height of his career. He was the foremost example of that prestige and power which an imperial knight could achieve within the empire. His services and those of his followers were eagerly sought after by the princes and even by the emperor. Also he was a wealthy man, and used his money in loans to the greater lords to further his own position and power. The power of Sickingen then rested not alone on military matters, but also on financial and economic. His greatness had been achieved through his ability to conserve and to increase the family inheritance. He knew how to sell his services to the highest bidder. And he had gained an excellent reputation among his fellow Free Knights and among the mercenaries who thus entrusted themselves to his leadership. During the campaign against the Duke of Württemberg, Hutten was completely won over to the side of Sickingen. In a letter to Erasmus, Hutten heaped praises on this imperial knight: "Franz is a man such as Germany had not had for many a day and who deserves to be immortalized in your letters. My hope is that great glory will accrue to our land through this man. Nothing which we admire in the ancients does he fail studiously to imitate. He is wise and persuasive, grapples with every situation with the alacrity and the indefatigability of a genuine leader. Nothing does he say or do in a servile manner, and at the moment he had a grand enterprise underway."[4]

In March, 1519, the campaign against the Duke began. With Sickingen and the forces of the Swabian League arrayed against him the duke was helpless. The campaign was a success. The honor of the Hutten clan had been upheld and had been avenged. These two men then turned themselves to the events about to begin at Worms. They considered that the German monk, Martin Luther, was the hope of Germany. However, the Diet of Worms blasted Hutten's hope that Luther would become the leader of a nationalist movement in Germany. "When the emperor and princes failed and Luther further receded from politics, Hutten fell back on Sickingen and his order of knights."[5] The knights then with Sickingen and Hutten as leaders were to bring about the reform of the empire which would place the German lands once more in their rightful position. However, the position of the knights was beginning to deteriorate. Under the new emperor Charles V, Sickingen had accepted a post as a general in the imperial war against the kingdom of France. But the campaign went against Sickingen. His lack of success caused the prestige and fortune so laboriously built up to decline rapidly. One unsuccessful campaign was enough to lose prestige as far as military matters were concerned. Not only was his military star on the wane, but his financial position too was serious. To help finance the imperial coronation, Sickingen had loaned some 20,000 gulden. However, this enormous sum had not been repaid promptly. In order to retain his fortune and prestige, Sickingen decided to begin the fateful campaign against the Archbishop of Trier.

Richard of Greiffenklau, elector and archbishop of Trier, was suspected of having been a supporter of Francis I of France in the recently held imperial elections, and it was also believed that the archbishop was an active opponent of Martin Luther. A successful campaign against the archbishop would thus accomplish three aims:

1. Give satisfaction to the personal enmity between Sickingen and Richard of Greiffenklau.

2. Eliminate an opponent of Luther and provide a wonderful coup d'etat for promoting the Gospel.

3. Rally the Free Knights together for the necessary reform of the empire.

After necessary preparations, the knights took the field in August, 1522. Four weeks later the attack on Trier was abandoned as hopeless. The forces of the archbishop were too strong. Richard of Greiffenklau had received the support of Philip of Hesse and Elector Ludwig of the Palatinate, who both had offered to provide foot soldiers, cavalry, and the equipment including the seige guns for the war against the knights. When the attack by the knights failed, Sickingen had to retreat. However, he made a costly strategic error, an error which was forced upon him by circumstances and the nature of his own forces. The knights of the Upper Rhineland were united in their war against the princes, and they had elected Sickingen as their captain. Now that the attack on Trier had failed, Franz felt that it was necessary to protect the lands and castles of all the knights in his army. Instead of taking refuge at his strongest fortress, the Ebernburg, Sick-ingen scattered his forces, in an attempt to protect all the knights' holdings. This was a crucial mistake.

The united princes were determined to deal with the knights in such a manner that never again would they pose a threat to their power. One by one the individual castles of the knights were smashed and were surrendered by the besieged inhabi-tants. Sickingen had taken refuge in the castle of Landstuhl, not the strongest of the fortresses. The castle was surrounded on three sides by the princes, and it suffered a terrific bombardment. Franz knew that the castle could not hold out without aid, and he knew that no aid was forthcoming. During one particularly heavy bombardment a shell struck a pile of lumber near Sick-ingen. A flying piece of timber hit the knight in the side, tearing a gaping hole. He was then moved to an underground passage. Since it was evident that the castle could not hold out, a capi-tulation was arranged. Sickingen was already dying. After Land-stuhl, the princes moved from castle to castle in a ruthless mop-ping-up campaign. The strongest of the fortresses was the Ebern-burg.[6] Sickingen's friend, Schenk Ernst von Tautenberg, had taken charge of the Ebernburg. The castle was located on a high hill. Tautenberg was determined to hold out and not surrender. He was in a very strong position with adequate resources in-cluding food and munitions. However, after a fierce five-day bombardment, this castle also capitulated. The day of the castle was over. The Knights' Revolt demonstrated this beyond a shadow of a doubt. Even the most obstinate had to accept the fact after the surrender of the Ebernburg.

Fortunately for Ulrich von Hutten, he had been ill during the revolt and had been unable to participate in the campaign against Trier. With the retaliation of the princes against the knights, Hut-ten fled to Switzerland.[7] He hoped that he would be safe from the revengeful supporters of the archbishop. He first sought sanc-tuary in Basel with Erasmus, but the Dutch man of letters re-fused to shelter him. Hutten was so angry that he wrote *An Ex-position* which was a bitter attack on Erasmus, accusing him of being a turncoat, a coward, and a betrayer of the true religion.[8] Erasmus was so influential, however, that he was able to get the town council of Basel to expel Hutten. Hutten then sought refuge with Zwingli in Zurich. Even then Erasmus wrote to the Zurich town council against the warrior, advising the council to refuse shelter to this man. But by this time Hutten was dead. On 29 August 1523, Ulrich von Hutten died on the island of Ufnau in Lake Zurich.

It is interesting to note Luther's reaction during this abortive uprising of the knights in Germany. These were the very men who had looked to him as the champion of German nationalism; as the man who would lead the fight to remove the abuses which both the papacy and the princes had been visiting upon Germany. Both Hutten and Sickingen were literally beside themselves with excitement when it became known that this German monk had been summoned to appear before the imperial diet at Worms. Both were equally afraid for Luther's safety and even for his life. Sickingen offered Luther haven should he have to flee Saxony.[9] While the arrangements were being made for Luther's arrival in Worms, the higher authorities tried to arrange things so that he would not have to make an appearance before an assemblage of the diet. Glapion, father-confessor to Emperor Charles V, even went to Sickingen's headquarters at the Ebernburg, in an attempt to arrange a meeting with Luther privately so as to avoid a public spectacle and perhaps avoid disturbances in Worms. Luther was to be brought to the Ebernburg for a private hearing, and of course, would receive the protection of Hutten and Sickingen. For their part, Sickingen was to be rewarded with a command under the emperor, and Hutten would receive some other suitable gift for him. But Luther refused these offers as we know. In fact, he declined all offers of protection before the meeting at Worms, and reluctantly accepted the refuge at the Wartburg from Frederick the Wise. However, he realized that for his own sake as well as for the safety and security of the position of the Elector of Saxony, it would be prudent to disappear for awhile.

If the knights led by Sickingen and Hutten expected to receive any help from Luther during their revolt, they were sadly mistaken. The mighty pen of the Reformer was not used to support this revolt against the legally constituted authority of the princes. But Luther did not bitterly attack the knights either, as he did the peasants in 1525. When he first received reports of the campaign against Trier he stated: "This affair will have a very bad ending."[10] Having preached against revolt in quieting the Wittenberg disturbances a few months earlier, Luther was merely being consistent in his attitude toward rebels of all kinds. He felt that God's justice would ultimately prevail and that the rebels would be destroyed. When he learned of Sickingen's death, a not too pleasant end for any man, he said, "God is a just and wonderful judge."[11]

Actually the Knights' Revolt was a rather minor affair in the life of Martin Luther. As Preserved Smith states in his work, *Age of the Reformation,* "It soon became apparent that all orders and all parts of Germany were in a state of ferment. The next manifestation of the revolutionary spirit was the rebellion of the knights."[12] It was in effect one more piece of evidence that there was social, economic, and political unrest in Germany, which was affecting all classes of people within the empire. Luther was really on the sidelines during the revolt. He took no part in it whatever. He neither supported the knights nor did he attack them as he was to do later with respect to the peasants and the Peasant Revolt in 1525. Luther didn't believe that legally constituted authorities were in any real danger. The allies of the archbishop of Trier were far too strong for the knights. He could feel sorry for Hutten and Sickingen. After all they had offered to aid him during his period of trial in 1521. But he really didn't owe them anything, and he certainly could not condone what they were attempting to do. Since the knights had no chance for success, there was no reason to fulminate against them. Time and God's justice would prevail.

However, there are other considerations for Luther's seeming disinterestedness. He was still consolidating his position after his return from the Wartburg, which occurred in March, 1522; and the knights had begun their campaign only a few months later, in August. He had a lot to do after being absent for over a year, and he was just too busy to concern himself with something he considered wrong. Furthermore, legally constituted authorities could cope with these uprisings.

The really important factor concerning Luther, however, was that his program of reform was essentially spiritual. R. H. Fife in his book *The Revolt of Martin Luther* sums up the situation rather well when he says: "Into this international game (the Diet of Worms) there intruded two powerful movements among the German people: The national resentment over the abuses in the Church, and the heresy of Luther. If these movements could have been united under the leadership of the sovereign, the future political and religious history of Germany would have been very different. That they were not united at Worms lay partly in the character of Luther himself, whose program was essentially spiritual, despite his appeal to the nobility, and partly in the character of Charles."[13]

Luther as pastor and teacher and after 1517 as leader of a reform movement was forced to write on many matters and subjects. His political ideas were never really paramount in his thinking. Even the famous Address to the Christian Nobility can be considered not only spiritual but essentially in form a sermon, not some kind of political testament. Luther had no real interest or knowledge in the vagaries and intricacies of politics of the 16th century, or of any century for that matter.

Even after their defeat, they remained for the most part supporters of the Lutheran cause. Although Luther had given them no support, he had not condemned them either. And the reader can question seriously whether the knights really did look to Luther for political leadership.

The knights, at least those directly involved in the Trier fiasco, were soundly defeated. Philip of Hesse, the future great Protestant political leader, played an important role in their defeat. It is very doubtful whether anyone in 1523 really realized that the defeat of the knights was the beginning of the end for the knightly class in the Germanies. It was this as time was to tell, but the ramifications of the defeat were simply not known at the time.

3.

THE PEASANTS IN A CHANGING SOCIETY: A BRIEF SURVEY

One of the most widespread of peasant uprisings occurred during the formative period of the early Reformation. In order to understand the so-called Peasants' War of 1525, it is necessary to recognize some of the changes which were taking place in the society of 16th-century Germany. Although this is by no means meant as a history of the 16th-century peasantry, it is essential that some attention be paid to the following: changes in the European economy; the introduction of Roman Law; the invention of and widespread use of the printing press; and the changing attitude of the peasant class itself. It is the peasant response to these factors which can help to explain the revolt of 1525. However, in view of the time period, it is also essential that some attention be paid to a pre-reformation peasant uprising where the stimuli of a Martin Luther is absent.

We know that there is generally too great a tendency to highlight the poor or miserable conditions of peasant life in 16th-century Europe. Actually, their lot had improved somewhat as a result of tremendous economic changes. Historians have emphasized the extremely heavy manorial duties and services imposed upon the peasant serf. It is said that he was little more than a slave being driven to work in his lord's fields by a brutal overseer with a whip; and that he had to spend so much time in his lord's fields that he could only work his own meager plot by moonlight.[1] No one can deny that there were hardships and that the duties at times were a great burden. But these facts alone were not enough to have caused such a widespread revolt. After all, conditions under which the peasant lived and worked varied greatly in Europe as a whole and in Germany in particular.

For about a century and a half Germany and Europe generally

24

had been undergoing very significant economic transformations. The basis of wealth was changing. In medieval times the basis of wealth was land. A man's wealth was not measured in terms of guldens or talers, but in the amount of land he owned or controlled. By the 16th century this was less true. Both trade and manufacturing had entered the picture. This is not meant to imply that there had been no trade or manufacturing before the 14th century. There had been fairs, and important cities had arisen at the intersection of trade routes. But generally speaking there were few towns before the 14th century which could be ranked as cities, and trade was really a very minor part in Europe's overall economy. Certainly, peasants as a class were little affected by these local fairs. The European economy was almost completely, and significantly, agricultural. Manufacture which had developed was for the most part for local consumption. The products of the craftsmen in the towns had a very limited sale geographically. The peasants came into the towns and exchanged their produce for necessities. However, in the 14th century trade and manufacturing became of increasing importance for the economy, and as a social force. The formation of the Hansa was one of the starting points. A new class was being formed—the merchant-trader class. Gradually, the peasant found that he had to compete with other people.[2] The manufacturer or tradesman in town might now sell his products to a commercial firm, and if the peasant wanted a particular product, his bid would have to be higher.

As important as the increased trade and manufacture were to the economy, their consequences were even more important to peasant life. Two important results came about because of this changing economy; namely, seizure of the commons by the nobility and the transition from direct barter to a monetary exchange. The peasants in reality had been members of a separate and quite distinct class. They lived pretty much by themselves, apart from the life of the towns. The peasant village was rather crude, in places even fortified after a fashion with a group of houses surrounded by a wall of stakes or a stockade having a rather narrow entrance, and at times even a deep ditch or moat surrounding the wall to deter marauders or the robber knights from entering. Every peasant had his own plot or more often a series of plots to work, which were not owned by the peasant himself, but rather by the lord who rented out the land in return for certain services and dues. However, there was some land which the peasant village held in common, such as streams, woods, and meadows. These holdings were not just important to the economy of the village—they were vital for its very existence. Take them away, and the village would be destitute. Thus when the commons began to be appropriated by the nobles or their use restricted by various laws, a real burden and grievance was placed upon the peasant. He began to regard his lord and protector with a different attitude. "The German peasant of 1525, like the French peasant of 1789, no longer looked up to his lord as his ruler and protector, but viewed him as a sort of legalized robber who demanded a share of his precious harvest, whose officers awaited the farmer at the crossing of the river to claim a toll, who would not let him sell his produce when he wished or permit him to protect his fields from the ravages of the pigeons which pleased the lord to keep."[3]

Seizure of the commons by members of the nobility had as a result the dispossessing of large numbers of peasants. The only place to which these unfortunates could go was the rapidly growing cities where they proceeded to form a group of unskilled labor ripe for revolt when the time was right. As will be shown later, the towns, too, took an active part in the Peasants' War of 1525, and this newly arrived element joined forces with the peasants. The basis used for seizure of the commons was of course the gradually introduced Roman Law which will be discussed shortly.

But this rise of a business and commercial class in the cities also brought about a need for monetary exchange. Certainly direct barter could not continue in a business economy. Something more efficient and less bulky was needed. Hence there came bills of credit and money exchange. But again the peasant was caught in the middle. Now everything was purchased in terms of money, of which the peasant had precious little. Great banking houses like the Fuggers arose, and these families and institutions played a tremendous role in the economic and even political life of central Europe. Although the following quotation is an illustration of ecclesiastical abuse, it also shows very clearly the importance of money at this time: "I see, said a Spaniard, that we can scarcely get anything from Christ's ministers but for money; at baptism money, at bishoping money, at marriage money, for confession money—no, not extreme unction without money! They will ring no bells without money, no burial in the church without money; so that it seemeth that Paradise is shut up from them that have no money. The rich is buried in the church, the poor in the churchyard. The rich may marry with his nearest kin, but the poor not so, albeit he be ready to die for love of her. The rich may eat flesh in Lent, but the poor may not, albeit fish be perhaps much dearer. The rich may readily get large Indulgences, but the poor none, because he wanteth money to pay for them."⁴

As a result of these really tremendous economic upheavals, Europe underwent changes which reached from the very top level of society right down the scale to the lowly peasant. The peasant could not but be affected by such changes, and as welcome as perhaps many were which raised his standard of living, there were still many which were a definite burden and which caused him to harbor a deep resentment against all who were not peasants: members of the nobility, the higher clergy, and the rich burghers in the towns. The peasant was a very conservative individual and change was unwelcome to him generally. Perhaps in the long run he would benefit tremendously, but he was more interested in the present, and he was experiencing these hardships now. That was the deciding factor.

The second main point in this changing and already changed Europe of the 16th century was the introduction of Roman Law. Roman Law which was certainly not new to the empire was nevertheless only gradually introduced into the rural and more remote areas, particularly in the German lands. The Old Germanic or Native Common Law was still widespread and provided the basic law under which the peasant lived. It was the practice under the Native Law for the peasant to be brought before a court where he was known. His fellow farmers or representatives of the village community sat in judgment. Naturally this was true where only minor infringements of the law were concerned. The Baurenmeister, those elected representatives of the peasant village, might form such a group. The important factor, however, was that he was not a stranger to these people. Even if the offense was serious, his lord, whom he knew, sat in judgment. But in the new courts under Roman Law, the whole atmosphere was different; it was almost impersonal. A learned judge heard the case. The peasant did not know him nor the judge the peasant. And it was better if the peasant could be represented by a lawyer or someone who had a decent knowledge of the new law. The personal element was removed, and the peasant felt this deeply. Before this change he felt that his case would be fairly heard since the court was composed of men like himself who recognized the difficulties and peculiarities of rural living. Everything was now strange to him: the people involved and the whole procedure. For an individual like the peasant who seldom ventured far from his farm or community, an appearance before the new court with all the pomp and ceremony and solemnity, was an experience that even frightened him. Whether real or imaginary, the new law system provided a psychological obstacle to the peasant.

But an even more important factor and certainly a very concrete one was the fact that Roman Law recognized only private property. Such a concept imperiled the commons of the village community which had been shared by all in the old Germanic tradition. "Since the right of the peasants were mainly unwritten, handed down by oral traditions, they were easily overridden by the bold and unscrupulous overlords."[5] This had the unfortunate effect, from the peasant viewpoint at least, of driving many from the country into the city. Naturally, not all lords were *bold* and *unscrupulous*. But we must remember that in a time when the basis of wealth was changing from land to trade and manufacturing, the landed proprietor was being forced into certain measures over which he had no control. He had to increase the efficiency of his farms and to consolidate for purely economic reasons. The towns, rapidly becoming cities, were squeezing the landed noble into a new position, and he didn't like this either, but there was little else that could be done. The rising burghers of the towns, the bankers and the traders, were forming an economic nobility; land was now being forced to produce, and to produce efficiently. More land could be cultivated with less labor, and so the commons were the first target of many landowners. They were incorporated into larger holdings with fewer workers. Those peasants no longer needed were forced into the towns; and, they became the nucleus of a new group of unskilled laborers who were quickly affected by any economic changes.

As important as the tremendous economic changes were and as important as the introduction of Roman Law or the transition from Native Law to Roman Law, one other factor should be emphasized. This was the changing psychological attitude of the peasant toward himself and perhaps more important toward the world generally. The peasant class as a whole began to recognize their own increased importance in the life of Europe.[6] Aware of this economic importance, they began to demand equality with other groups. They considered that not only was their vocation just as important as that of the trader or banker (perhaps more since they were producers), but the results of their work were just as important. People still had to eat. As a result of this feeling, they objected and at times quite strongly to the imposition of social and economic conditions which they considered marks of unequal status. How could they be so inferior when their work and the results of this work were so vital to the life of Europe? Naturally, they didn't consider Europe generally, but in their own immediate environs, they knew of their own importance. Yet they were considered on such a low level socially as to have no status whatever. At times the livestock were more important than they were.

"In poetry, play, and song the peasant was pictured as stupid, obscene, nasty, scheming, stubborn, gluttonous, and hard-drinking, little above the level of an animal. The minnesingers loved to ridicule him in court entertainments. The burghers of the town made him the butt of their coarse jokes. Contemporary artists treated him more kindly, portraying him as he really was, not the degraded, depraved individual presented in literature."[7] No one could remain unaffected by such treatment. Picture a peasant brought before his lord holding court. The lord's followers would begin to laugh when they first caught sight of him. A court minstrel would sing a ditty about this coarse boor standing in front of them. When he went into town on one of his very infrequent visits, he was laughed at and ridiculed practically as soon as he entered the gate. He was either an animal to be laughed at or a person of such low caste as to be completely ignored.

However, a very real change began to occur in the 15th century, and perhaps the introduction of the printing press might be given some of the credit for expediting this change. One of the main features of the pre-Lutheran reform movements was the emphasis on the return to primitive Christianity, the necessity to imitate Christ and to adopt the life lived by the early Apostles and followers of Christ. These were the true Christians, and in order to live a Christian life, one had to emulate the life, including the dress and work of these early Christians. Primitive Christianity seemed to be a main and dominant theme. But there was a class of individuals already living in Europe who lived a very simple life, worked hard, expected little reward, dressed and ate simply, and in many respects seemed to coincide closely with the ideas that some writers had about the Apostles. The lowly peasant, so scorned by many, was now compared to the early Apostles. He did not dress in rich garments and make a show of his wealth. He was a simple man of the soil, a man living primitive Christianity.

Quite suddenly and miraculously the peasant was vicariously endowed with a marvelous education and intellect so that he was not only competent but quite able to discuss the works of Erasmus, Luther, and other scholars who wrote on theological matters. This transition from one extreme to the other was astounding; perhaps the two existing side by side was even more important. "Such a peasant did not exist, but the psychological effect on his brothers was immeasurable. They readily believed that they were destined to perform an important role in furthering the Gospel, and incidentally, in inaugurating much-needed social and economic reform."[8]

Peasant revolts in Europe were common occurrences before the days of Luther. The Bundschuh revolts of 1493 may be regarded as typical. First, and rather important, was the fact that the peasants and townsmen (the lower class) combined for a time in a common effort, and this fact is a common feature of these uprisings. In reality, these movements could be more properly designated as revolts of the lower classes, generally against the upper; as revolts of the debtor against the creditor. So both the lower class of the towns and the peasants of the country were involved. It is true, however, that the peasants provided the bulk in numbers. Generally only a small number in the towns joined forces with the rural folk.

The peasant's shoe, tied with a string, or Bundschuh, was the symbol or standard of revolt. Often there was merely a bundschuh hoisted aloft on a pole as a banner. Some groups provided themselves with a more elaborate symbol; such a one was made of blue silk with a white cross in the center with a picture of the crucified Christ. On one side of Christ there was a bundschuh; on the other side there was a kneeling peasant. The patron saints were the Virgin and St. John. These revolts or uprisings occurred sporadically throughout southern Germany in the 15th century. None reached large proportion. Their importance lies more in their frequency than in the area affected or in the results. They were very quickly suppressed since as shown in the revolt of 1525, peasant bands were no match for the soldiery of the nobility.

For the most part their aims and demands were economic with a sprinkling of political and religious demands. But the main point is that economic conditions were the prime impulse in these uprisings. Some of their general aims were to cancel all debts; reduce tolls and taxes; replace imperial courts of law with native courts; control the income of the priests; destroy the usurious

Jews; abolish auricular confession; declare water, forests, and pasture lands the common property of all; and recognize no lord but the Emperor.[9]

The plan was to rally the peasants of all Germany and with the assistance of the townspeople to achieve deliverance from their oppressors. It is interesting to note that the movement in Alsace hoped to receive aid from the Swiss, but this was not forthcoming. One can see from an examination of the above demands that some were economic, and all refer to abuses which had come about as a result of the changing economic conditions in Europe. One important feature of these demands which reappears in the movement of 1525 is no lord but the emperor. The peasants had no intention of upsetting the head of the empire, but they were willing to swear allegiance only to him. It was the local nobility that were squeezing them. There were too many intermediaries or obstacles between the emperor and his subjects. Even in Germany, where nationalism was beginning to rise, there was objection to the power of the local nobility.

Roman Law and its consequences are evident in the demands which are covered in earlier pages of this introduction and were of vital importance to the life of the peasant and to the peasant village. These old rights were being usurped by the local lord, and there had to be a return to the old customs and traditions. Controlling the income of the priests was both economic and religious since as quoted before, money exactions were levied for practically everything including confession. The lower class saw beside its own increasing poverty a wealthy and prosperous clergy, living in luxury and wealth seemingly out of proportion to its parishioners. Exactions of the Church were becoming too great.

The above has been a brief survey attempting to show some of the changing economic conditions which were a feature of the 16th century, and to show the peasants' role in all of this. The change from barter to a money economy coupled with the rise of towns and the increasing importance of trade and manufacturing in the economic life of Europe placed the peasant class in a very precarious financial position. Whether these conditions were only temporary was of little concern to the peasant at the time. He only recognized the increased taxes and burdens which were placed upon him. The transition to Roman Law changed the very basis of property holding in Germany, and resulted in a gradual dislocation of many peasant families. All of these factors brought a not too subtle psychological change in the peasant's basic attitude toward his lord and those about him. He now considered that he, as a producing member of society and as a very important factor in the economy, should be getting some of the benefits of the increasing wealth so evident around him.

4.

THE WAR: A SURVEY

The first event which led to the Peasants' War[1] occurred in the summer of 1524 on the lands of the Count of Lupfen near Stühlingen on the outskirts of the Black Forest. The immediate cause for the disturbance arose from the demand by the countess that the peasants pick berries and snail shells during harvest time. This might seem to have been an innocuous reason for the beginning of a revolt which swept over most of southern Germany. However, whenever unjustified demands or requests were made upon the peasants by their lord, it was often common practice for these peasants to join together and appoint a deputation which would then present their grievances to the noble involved. Such was undoubtedly the case at Stühlingen. Surely one can visualize the consternation and perhaps anger of these tillers of the soil who had been asked (which in effect was really a demand) to take off time from their harvest activities to pick berries for the countess. There must have been at least one outspoken farmer who voiced his indignation and who was able to influence his fellow tenants. After all they had precious little time as it was to devote to their own work. They felt that they already performed enough duties and services for the count, and perhaps in the unwritten agreement between count and peasant concerning these dues and services, harvest time and church holidays were exempt from service to their lord. By August, 1524, a band of some one thousand peasants had been formed under the leadership of the former Landsknecht, Hans Müller. To the lowly peasant who ventured little from his own farm, Müller must have been a glamorous figure. He was a man of the world, a man who had travelled, who had fought as a professional soldier, who knew how to deal with the nobility and was not afraid of standing up for his rights. As the group of discontented peasants moved, it was joined by others until the ranks were swelled enormously. The movement spread to Upper Swabia and Württemburg, where a new element was added. Duke Ulrich of Württemburg at this time was under the imperial ban. Such a gathering of peasants seemed to provide just the necessary weapon for him to regain his lands and hereditary rights. However, the Duke was unsuccessful. Near Stuttgart, the Duke's forces were routed by the forces of the Swabian League, and the Duke was forced to take refuge in the Castle of Hohentwiel.

One of the main features of German history at this time was the existence of various leagues of cities. The Swabian League and the Hansa are such examples. In times of crisis a league could muster military forces for its protection. This gave it strong bargaining power with the German princes, and considerable influence in German political life. But the Swabian League could not cope with the whole movement at one time. A contagion was spreading, or so it seemed. Various groups of discontented peasants appeared to arise everywhere, and in a helter-skelter manner. There was not yet a definite plan. One minute the Swabian League was faced with one band, the next minute there were twenty or so. The mere spontaneity of the movement disrupted any possible concerted action by the authorities. The element of surprise was indeed important. For the authorities were surprised at the speed of the movement. In the past such movements as the *Arme Conrad* or the *Bundschuh* were fairly local in character and extent. The range of their activities was fairly limited, and the authorities could easily cope with the situation. But by the end of 1524 almost all of southern Germany was aflame. "Reports from Franconia, Hesse, Brunswich, Baden, Treves, Salzburg, Thuringia, Tyrol, Carinthia, and Styria all indicated that the local princes were faced with civil war. The worst region was Thuringia where Münzer and his followers had preached violence and defiance of all accepted authority as the only means to the new order."[2] It seems ironic perhaps that the locale of Luther's birthplace should be the scene of the most bitter episodes of the whole war. The man who preached disapproval of violence and revolt against lawfully constituted authority saw his native Thuringia aflame. One perhaps can speculate as to the influence which this may have had on Martin Luther.

One important factor must be strongly emphasized in any study of the Great Peasants' War: there was no overall plan of action or unity within the peasant movement. In fact, each group of peasants presenting its demands to the local lords acted as a separate and distinct unit. The broad scope of the movement does not prove organization, central direction, or uniform objectives. The Peasants' War was in reality a series of local disturbances which at times resulted in very bitter fighting, and which unfortunately arose throughout the greater part of southern Germany at about the same time. The peasants had the advantage of surprise and spontaneity; of overwhelming numbers; and, in some cases the assistance of townsmen.

The element of surprise is a very important factor, and the peasants were able to achieve some element of surprise at least in the early stages of the war. The local lord might have some forewarning of a gathering of peasants, but such gatherings had occurred in the past, and problems had always been solved. It was the size of this movement and the astonishing speed with which it grew that surprised the princely group. In the past there had been enough time to prepare for serious uprisings, but not this time. In many cases, depending on the size of the noble's holdings, there were spontaneous meetings throughout his lands.

The nobles soon realized that they could not possibly cope with a situation which had become so widespread and seemed so serious.

In numbers alone the peasants were far superior, and it is not surprising that the princely ranks were afraid and considered that very evil days had befallen them. There was one policy they could follow which might at least stave off the final reckoning for a time. They could be conciliatory and thus buy time. They could give in on minor points, and agree to talk things over on the more serious demands presented to them. They had to have time in order to prepare for the eventual overthrow of this god-less movement. The nobles found that they had very inadequate forces at their disposal in the beginning of the revolt. The Italian Wars of Charles V had depleted Germany of its best-trained fighting men. A policy of wait and see was definitely called for under the circumstances. Little could be done until responsible leaders assembled to decide upon a policy, and until adequate forces gathered to meet the threat. It would be folly to rush into a struggle with the great mass of peasants until preparations were complete. Otherwise a real disaster might occur. One out-standing advantage of the princes was that they did have the leaders who were capable of putting down the revolt. Truchess of the Swabian League was a seasoned campaigner, and an able general and professional soldier. In the last analysis it was a question of who would win: the professional soldiers of the princes or untrained mobs of peasants. There could be little doubt of the outcome. A group of peasants, regardless of its size, could accomplish little against a well-trained, well-equipped, well-disciplined, and well-led force. The peasants in many cases fled from the battlefield at the sight of approaching cavalry with swords and lances shining in the sunlight.

So where the peasants originally had surprise, numbers, and support of townsmen on their side, the princes had time, which they bought at the expense of the peasants, and a well-trained army which proved to be more than a match for the mob. But enough of the peasant army versus the princely ranks. As has been mentioned above, the lower classes in the towns did feel an affinity for the peasant cause, and in some cases did join forces with the peasants. Rothenburg is a good example of this, and there is a fairly full account of Rothenburg's role in the Peasants' War.[3] In the main the documents available are a collection of minutes of the city council, and the agenda, petitions, resolutions passed, and diplomatic correspondence between Rothenburg and other communities. Rothenburg had a rather special place in German political life at the time in that it was a free city of the Reich.[4] Its authority extended to a considerable distance outside the walls of the town covering many villages and hamlets; and, of course, there were many peasants who owed their allegiance, dues, and services to this Free City. The secretary of the city council kept a detailed and full account of Rothenburg's role in the Peasants' War.

The first teachings of the new movement called the Reformation were brought to Rothenburg by Dr. Johannes Deuschlin, Hans Schmidt, and Kaspar Cristan. However, it wasn't until 1524 that a really important figure arrived, and one intimately associated with the new teaching, Karlstadt, or Andreas Rudolphus Bodenstein. By 1524 he had already broken with Luther, having left Wittenberg the year before. His name was known throughout Germany, and by 1524 he was considered by many to be a dangerous individual who should be avoided. Rothenburg provides an example of this attitude. The city council considered his presence in the city dangerous to the maintenance of authority, and an edict was passed in council ordering his expulsion from the city and from the surrounding territory controlled by Rothenburg. The edict was not passed, however, without some outside pressure. Margrave Casimir of Ansbach, who looked with rather covetous eyes on the city, deemed it wise and necessary that Karlstadt, the rabble rouser, be forced to leave. But the edict was never carried out. Karlstadt had gone into hiding, which was most convenient for all concerned, because there certainly must have been many citizens who were followers of the famous scholar.

On March 21, 1525, the first overt act of the Peasants' War occurred in Rothenburg. A band of about 30 peasants, accom-

panied by fife and drum, marched into the city. One can imagine
the sight presented to the city council and burghers of the Free
City. The council ordered their immediate withdrawal. There was
no violence or disturbance. The peasants simply walked out of
the gate. They were not daunted or overawed by the treatment
they had received, but it was a strange beginning for a war. A
meeting was then scheduled at Ohrenbach, where all peasants
possible were to assemble with available arms. The odd assort-
ment of weapons carried by those who came was far inferior to
those of the forces of the princes.

When word of the assembly reached the inner city council of
Rothenburg, the good citizens were quite alarmed. A messenger
was immediately dispatched to the peasants with a severe repri-
mand from the council, and with orders to disband and quietly
go home. In defiance, the peasants seized the messenger, but
released him after twenty-four hours without harm. This act
alone was defiance of the council's authority and a blow to its
prestige. When Margrave Casimir was informed of these events,
he immediately offered his good services to quell the revolt for
Rothenburg. The margrave was looking for such an opportunity
to gain control of the city, but such action had to be undertaken
through strictly legal means. If the city were to ask for his aid
and protection, he would automatically gain control of it. Needless to say, his offer was rejected at this time. The peasants
meanwhile had drawn up a list of demands and submitted them
to the council, but before any action could be taken on these
demands, a serious situation arose within the town itself. A split
had occurred between the council on the one hand, and the
burghers on the other. Nürnberg, Schwäbisch Hall and Dunkels-
bühl all offered to act as mediators in this internal affair, and this
offer was likewise rejected. The good citizens of the Free City
wanted to solve their own problems without any outside inter-
ference, if possible. The burghers having formed a committee of
their own, presented their grievances to the town council. The
committee represented some 20 trades within Rothenburg, and
naturally it carried some weight. Their demands can be sum-
marized briefly as follows:

1. Scaling down of taxes.
2. Reforms in the administration of justice.
3. Reforms concerning the church and secularization of property.
4. Social reforms putting all citizens on an equal footing.
5. Reorganization of the city government, including election of a new representative council.

At this time the burghers also forced the council to open its books on the budget and expenditures. The committee's influence indeed must have been considerable for this to happen. In the meantime a liaison was established between the peasants and the burgher committee. Talks were held, and it was agreed that no action of any kind would be taken by either side for a period of three weeks, during which time the Rothenburg peasants could go to the aid of their brother groups nearby. But these groups would be under other jurisdictions, and not under Rothenburg. The committee was able almost completely to frustrate the authority of the council. Karlstadt came out of hiding, and the council could do nothing. In fact, the formal mandates made against him were withdrawn. Rothenburg was in the midst of a revolution.

The city's predicament was very real, and this was known elsewhere. As a result an imperial commission paid a visit with the view of mediating between the disputing parties within the city. Since Rothenburg was a Free City of the Reich with certain privileges, the commission had no real authority to force a solution. It could advise, but nothing else. The committee of burghers succeeded in almost completely ignoring even the presence of the imperial commission, and certainly did nothing to aid the commission in ascertaining the true facts of the situation. On 16 April 1525, a new constitution was formally ratified giving to the city a legal democratic form of government (perhaps a limited type of representative government would best describe the form). At any rate there was a very real victory for the burghers. They would now have a definite share in the city government. The power of the old council was broken.

Now the city council found itself in a very serious situation.

News of peasant atrocities, particularly at Weinsberg, reached Rothenburg. Many of the citizens became afraid of the whole affair. Their neutrality was slowly but surely being crushed between the peasants on the one hand and the forces of the Swabian League on the other. Margrave Casimir was tired of trifling and sought to force a showdown. The peasants for their part demanded that the city join their movement. Neutrality had no place in such a situation. The city was in a true dilemma. It was forced into a position of having to choose between the two, and it chose to support the peasant movement as the lesser of two evils. On 10 May 1525, just five days before the disastrous defeat at Frankenhausen, Rothenburg formally subscribed to the 12 articles. As long as the burgher committee was in partial control, and as long as the city was being governed under the new constitution, its position was firm and irrevocable. However, it was not long before the citizens realized, much to their sorrow, that they had picked the loser. With the defeat at Frankenhausen and subsequent peasant disasters, the whole peasant movement began to collapse. The conservative element in the city was quick to size up the situation. A counterrevolution within quickly restored the old government and constitution. Both the peasants and the burghers had lost.

Thus Rothenburg provides one example of the cooperation which did occur between the peasants and townsmen. In Rothenburg's case, no active assistance was given to the peasant movement, at least in a material sense. Perhaps if Rothenburg had not been a Free City, the Margrave would quickly have settled the situation, and the episode would have been a short one.

Let us now look closely at the demands of these various peasant groups. Grievances and demands were not uniform throughout the whole movement. Since the Peasants' War was an uncoordinated movement with each group of peasants acting almost completely independent of others, many different lists of demands were composed: some lists went into great detail concerning abuses which should be corrected to make peasant life more amenable. Some contained as many as 64 different articles. It is not necessary to examine all the known lists of the various peasants groups. It will suffice for the present study to examine in some detail the Twelve Articles of the Peasants of Swabia which can be considered representative of the demands presented by the peasants to the local lords.[5]

The war had begun in August, 1524, near Stühlingen, but it was not until March, 1525, that the famous Twelve Articles came into existence. Southern Germany had been divided into three main districts: Ried, Lake Constanz, and the Black Forest. These three districts did manage to achieve a unity of purpose of sorts, and were able to reach an understanding among themselves. The results of this understanding as to aims and policy were the Twelve Articles. A meeting of peasant leaders had been arranged at Memmingen for March, 1525, and the formal demands were then drawn up and adopted.

The foreword or introduction to the Twelve Articles opens with the phrase "Peace to the Christian Reader and the Grace of God through Christ." The foreword attacks those people who claim that the cause of the revolt was the new teaching. How can the Gospel be the cause of revolt and disorder when the Gospel is the message of Christ? The real disturbers of the peace, so says the foreword, are those people who refuse reasonable demands. The generalities comprising the foreword to the Twelve Articles place all the blame so to speak on the opposing side. The peasant movement is motivated only by the highest ideals; their demands, and let all examine them carefully, are in full accord with the teachings of Jesus. They are reasonable and just. The foreword is then followed by the main list:

1. The community should have the power and authority to choose and appoint its own pastor with the right to depose him.

2. The peasants are willing to pay a just tithe. A church provost, appointed by the community, should collect this. From this tithe a sufficient sum should be given to the elected pastor; the rest should be given to the poor. Provision should be made for those people forced to leave the community, due to poverty and lack of jobs. No improper tithes will be paid.

3. Men should be free and not considered property of another.

4. They should be allowed to fish and hunt; which right did not belong to the privileged alone.

5. They should have access to woods and be allowed to cut timber.

6. Excessive imposition of services should cease.

7. They should be free from oppression in the form of unspecified services.

8. There should be a readjustment of rents.

9. The constant making of new laws being a burden, all cases should be judged according to their merits.

10. Enclosing and expropriation of the commons being an evil, they should be reopened.

11. The *Todfall* should be abolished.

12. If these articles were not in agreement with God's Word, let them be changed when proven so.

One can see from an examination of the above articles that economic demands predominated. Tithes, services, the commons were all mentioned, and these were all connected with real abuses which the peasants suffered. They were burning issues of the day. But there were also socio-political demands, particularly those involving freedom (no man should be the property of another). We should hesitate to read political freedom into this specific demand; social issues were far more important. The right to use woods and streams was primarily economic, but there was a social basis. Why should these areas be reserved for only one class of people? The woods and streams were actually needed by all men. The fruit of these areas provided a variety in diet for the peasant, and at times was of tremendous economic importance to him, especially in times of bad harvest. But the real issue was that they should be accessible to all men, not just the privileged few. And so it was with the question of serfdom. Did one man have the right to own another? Not all Germany had a rigid serfdom. Many of the people were free in body from their lords.

The peasant leaders felt that they had composed a fair list of demands, which reasonable people were able to accept with little or no reservations. But they did leave a way out for themselves. If these articles were not in agreement with the Word of God, they could be changed. Luther's reply to the Twelve Articles will be considered later.

Now let us turn to an examination of four representative leaders of the peasant movement. Two can be termed intellectual leaders (Münzer and Karlstadt); one was almost completely a military leader and one of the few peasant leaders who had any previous military experience (Florian Geyer); the last (Michael Gaismair) was unique in that his movement in the Tyrol outlasted any of the others, and continued right down to 1526. Even then Gaismair was not stopped until he had fled the scene.

Whenever one reads about the Peasants' War, he invariably comes across the name of Thomas Münzer.[6] If anyone can be considered either typical or representative of the intellectual forces within the peasant cause, Münzer is that person. Münzer was born in the last quarter of the 15th century, very close undoubtedly to the time of Luther's birth. His education was rather good for the time. His first known profession was that of a teacher in the Latin School at Aschersleben and then at Halle. In 1515 he was a confessor in a nunnery and then a teacher again at Brunswick. Up to 1520 Münzer's life was far from outstanding, and if it had not been for the events following 1520, it is doubtful whether the world would ever have had any interest in the man, or perhaps have even heard of him. But fame was to come to him. In the year 1520 he accepted a post as preacher at the Marienkirche in Zwickau, and here his life as a well-known public figure really began. He soon became associated with the Zwickau Prophets, and became as radical as they. He was now interested in mysticism, and poured over the works of such mystics as Meister Eckhardt and Johannes Tauler. Through his reading and contemplation he became convinced of the necessity of a thorough going revolution of Church and State. The church seemed filled with ungodly men, and it was spoiled by abuse. The State on the other hand was doing nothing about this deplorable situation. Something had to be done. The Zwickau Prophets only increased his mysticism and radicalism.

Up to 1520 Münzer might be considered a follower of Luther,

or at least a supporter of the Saxon Reformer. However, his radicalism drove him from Luther's path, and a break was inevitable. In 1521 he was forced to flee to Bohemia. He denounced the clergy. At Alstätt he conducted the entire church service in German. And here at Alstätt his views and opinions were crystallized into a clear-cut program. He believed that the primitive church was the basis for the Kingdom of God on earth. Freedom and equality of all should reign. Those people who refuse to espouse the new gospel should be overthrown. This was a direct call for revolt against any authority, lay or ecclesiastical, which refused to support the new teaching. Those who refused to become citizens of the Kingdom of God should either be banished or killed. Private wealth was to cease; property was to be held in common. Certainly if one is looking for a radical program among the peasants, here it is. No wonder the princes considered Münzer a loathsome person, to be destroyed at all costs. One can imagine the popular appeal he must have had among many elements of the population. And it is not hard to understand why Luther was also appalled at his radical program. Common ownership of all property was certainly counter to anything Luther believed. Freedom and equality for all was again a principle or doctrine which was contrary to all existing forms of government. Although his program was radical for the times, Münzer was a sincere man, and no one could deny the fact. He believed wholeheartedly in his program. The end of Thomas Münzer came with the defeat of the peasants at Frankenhausen. Münzer was able to escape, but only temporarily. He was captured, tortured, and finally executed. His end was as violent as his life had been since he had embarked on his program of revolution.

Another important figure in the Peasant Movement was Andreas Rudolphus Bodenstein, better known as Karlstadt. He was born just a little before Luther in the city of Karlstadt in Franconia, and hence his name. His first contact with Luther came in 1508 when the latter first taught at the University of Wittenberg. Karlstadt had previously studied in Italy, and was considered a scholar of the first rank. In 1510 he was made Professor of Theology and Archdeacon of the Collegiate Church in Wittenberg.[7] In 1515 he made a journey to Rome, and upon his return to the University found that the theology of Wittenberg was undergoing a change wrought by Martin Luther. At first Karlstadt resisted the change, but was soon won over to it, and became one of its great supporters. However, he went to extremes and also became a mystic. The year 1521 was momentous for this man. Luther was in hiding at the Wartburg, after appearing before the emperor at Worms. Karlstadt proceeded to take the lead in the reformation at Wittenberg, so that Luther, as we saw above, was forced to return because of the radical happenings in his home town. On January 20, 1522, Karlstadt married, and thus was one of the first to take this serious step in defiance of the monastic vows. In the spring of 1523 he left Wittenberg, and became a pastor at Orlamünde; in 1524 because of his teachings and public utterances, he was banished from Saxony. However, through the intervention of Luther in his behalf, he was able to return in 1526. He was kept under strict control, and was forbidden to preach or write for publication. In 1528 he fled Saxony because of the restrictions. He roamed throughout Friesland and the Rhine regions until 1530, when he arrived in Strasburg. During the debate between Luther and Zwingli, he supported Zwingli. In 1531 he was appointed pastor of Alstätten in the Rhineland, and in 1534 was made professor of theology at Basel. Here he died in 1541 as a result of the plague. Karlstadt was a remarkable figure in the history of the Reformation. He was an intelligent man, but certainly lacked stability. His chief fault lay in his inability to follow. He wanted to be the leader. There is no doubt that he was sincerely devoted to the cause of the Reformation. Unfortunately, he did not have the capacity to lead. When he did take the opportunity as in 1521 during Luther's absence, he went to extremes, and alienated many elements, especially Luther himself.

As for the military leaders among the peasants, they were very rare individuals. Military leadership and the art of war were for the most part advantages on the side of the princes and nobles. However, there were several exceptions to this, and one of them was in the person of Florian Geyer.[8] There were other skilled military leaders of the peasants, but Geyer and a few other Knights represent a case which is typical. He was a member of that fast declining class in the empire, the free knight. Much like von Sickingen, he was a minor land owner, and a member of the minor nobility. The plight of the knight was very real in this changing Europe.[9] He was in reality caught between the forces of the great nobles who were adapting themselves to the changing conditions, at the expense of their peasants, and the rising townsmen, who were beginning to form a sort of economic nobility. The knight was in most cases the proprietor of a rather small holding, with a few peasants, or perhaps none at all. He could not cope with the changing times, for there was no basis upon which he could make a change. The term "robber knight" was perhaps very accurate. Geyer had been the lord of the old castle of Giebelstadt near Würzburg. If it had not been for the Peasants' War, possibly the name of Geyer would have remained unknown. He might have taken up the profession of brigand in order to survive the new times. However, near the end of March, 1525, he suddenly appeared in the Tauber Valley to aid the peasant cause. It was at this time that he formed his famous Black Troop which became one of the most efficient fighting forces on the peasant side, and one that was a worthy match for the forces of General Truchess of the Swabian League. The Black Troop was well organized, well trained and well armed. In all battles in which it participated, it gave an excellent account of itself. But one troop of cavalry, even under an inspired leader, could not stop the forces of destruction for long. At Frankenhausen even Geyer's forces were overcome. But he did flee from the slaughter; later he was killed, near Schwäbisch Hall, and his troop was decimated. Geyer was the ideal type of hero who came rushing to aid the peasant cause, the cause of the underdog. He fought bravely and well, and remained a hero to the peasant.

Another interesting leader of the peasants was Michael Gaismair. His movement, which was centered in the Tyrol, lasted until well into 1526; and even after it collapsed, he remained a threat to the princes and the nobility. However, his ideas and program were fairly local in character, and remained almost completely a Tyrolese movement with little following outside this Alpine region.

Gaismair was born the son of a squire of Sterzing, and hence a member of that minor nobility, which although they had little real power did have land and prestige which put them far above the peasant class. He was a scholar of sorts who later seemed to reject all learning except for Biblical studies, and perhaps in this alone he might resemble the famous Karlstadt, who also had a tendency later on to scorn some scholarly pursuits. His opposition to learning except Biblical studies will be seen presently from an examination of his program. Gaismair had been secretary to the Bishop of Brixen and then keeper of the customs at Klausen. He had had the opportunity in both positions to acquaint himself with the conditions and peculiarities of the region. He proceeded to formulate a plan or program to correct what he considered to be the most obvious abuses in the life of the times. His program of reform consisted of five main points:

1. All fortifications and castles were to be destroyed.

2. The creation of one strong central government to administer public affairs was recommended.

3. One University was to be established at the seat of the Central Government; only Biblical studies were to be allowed.

4. There were to be no towns or villages.

5. All merchants were forbidden.

The above program was radical and anti-intellectual, and it is no wonder that it had such a small following outside the Tyrol. However, the concept of one strong central government was certainly not new, for the cry in the pre-1525 revolts often concerned no lord but the emperor, and point two was merely an echo of this sentiment. Actually it was opposition to the feudal regime with the many lords and nobles who all claimed authority in political and public affairs to various degrees. The destruction of castles and fortifications was an attempt to insure peace throughout the country. With each noble or prince having his own stronghold, peace was hard to maintain if the noble wished to dispute the point. One is reminded of the program of Louis XIV concerning the razing of castles and strongholds in order to assure tranquility throughout France.

Somewhere along the way Gaismair had acquired an anti-intellectual attitude and certainly the creation of only one university to be engaged only in Biblical studies reflects this. The lack of towns or villages and the prohibition against merchants was a reaction against all trade, and indicated a desire for a purely agricultural society. With all the people engaged on the land, with no towns or merchants, no fortifications, and the existence of only one seat of government, a Utopia was visualized. There was to be peace and harmony among all people which could be easily enforced if the above program were adopted.

As the revolt collapsed, and with his life in danger, Gaismair fled to Venice. He was one of the few leaders among the peasants who did not die on the field of battle or who were not executed after capture. However, the very fact that he still lived was a constant threat to the authorities in the eastern Alpine region. He could return at any time and foment another rebellion. In 1528, two years after his flight, he did return to Switzerland, but this time not as a leader of rebellion but in the capacity of a diplomat. He held the position as plenipotentiary for the Venetian Republic in dealings with Count Ulrich of Württemberg. One can imagine the consternation and even fear which his return must have engendered among the princely ranks. But his days as a popular leader in the Tyrol were over. There was no renewed outbreak of rebellion, and Gaismair returned to Venice unharmed. Sometime later in Padua, so the story goes, he was murdered by two Spanish assassins. It was a fitting end to a fabulous career.

One might well ask the question, what chance of success did the Peasant Movement have in gaining its objectives? What could such uncoordinated groups hope to accomplish by their rebellion? Was this whole affair a revolution or merely a rebellion of numerous groups of discontented elements within Germany (or the empire) which arose spontaneously but with no unity of command or purpose? It seems certain that the latter is the case.

First of all, there was no clear-cut program. Each peasant group presented its own separate list of demands. Even at Memmingen, the scene of the adoption of the Twelve Articles, the so-called Peasants' Parliament, there was no real unity. There were quarrels, and the Articles which became so famous were accepted only as a basis for negotiation with the princely ranks, and no group considered itself bound to the articles. In such areas as Alsace and the Tyrol as well as other places, the Twelve Articles were never adopted. Even in those areas where they were, the main aims were varied and just as diverse as the leaders themselves. Some groups wanted a peasant dictatorship, some a classless society, some a return of the old feudalism where everything was regulated by a contract between lord and peasant, and others wanted the abolition of all rulers except the Pope and the Emperor. Could there be either any chance of success or real unity so necessary to success when the objectives were so divergent? What if the peasants had succeeded? Would it not have been possible for a new war to have broken out between the peasants themselves as a result of their differing aims? Success seems very unlikely.

The leaders themselves provide an ample illustration of the diversity of the movement. Some of them were themselves peasants, others were former secretaries to ecclesiastics; there were scholars, and there were even knights, themselves members of the nobility. Hans Müller, Michael Gaismair, Thomas Münzer, and Florian Geyer were all leaders, and what a difference there was among these men! What did a peasant have in common with a man like Gaismair, former secretary to the Bishop of Brixen, or with Thomas Münzer, preacher and scholar?

The gulf which invariably existed between leader and follower too often revealed itself in lack of discipline: discipline in both battle and in time of victory after battle. For the main question is what was the follower, the simple peasant, really interested in gaining in the various actions and battles in the war? These hordes of simple land-tilling farmers were interested mainly in pillaging castles and cloisters, draining fish ponds, and raiding the game sanctuaries which had been reserved for the lords.

These were goals which they could understand. They might not have them for long, but at least temporarily they could indulge themselves. They could understand the objective of subduing a cloister, and the leader of the small band could encourage them with the value of plunder to be gotten from the action. In the early days of the war, before the nobles could take effective countermeasures, the so-called battles of the peasant groups were more often pillaging and looting forays, and little blood was shed. More heads were hurt from the wine than from any hard knocks of the opposing forces. But there was no discipline. Weinsberg remains a classic example where discipline completely broke down. Perhaps Rohrbach would not have received the hatred of the princes if he had ceased killing when ordered. There were exceptions of course, and Florian Geyer provides the exception to the rule with his famous Black Troop, but he is the exception.

The Twelve Articles might very well be considered moderate and reasonable, able to be conscientiously examined by the nobles as a basis for negotiation. But what of Münzer's program or even that of Gaismair? Could these programs be considered a basis for negotiation? No! They were to be accepted in toto. There was certainly no room in Münzer's program for discussion. Either they were accepted or rejected. If not accepted completely, the person involved was either to be banished or killed. There was not much choice.

The distinguishing features of the Peasants' War of 1525 from the earlier revolts already mentioned previously are really two-fold: first, the scope and extent of the rebellion in 1525 far exceeded anything before that time. Neither the Bundschuh nor the Arme Conrad had enveloped such a large area. Nor were such large numbers of people involved. The Peasants' War of 1525 certainly had none of the unity of the Puritan Revolution, but was in reality a series of Bundchuh revolts with the added factor of occurring all at one and the same time. The second factor was the existence of Luther and his teachings, which did have a great influence in the empire at the time and which naturally affected the various peasant groups in revolt. It is true that there was no religious unity within the peasant movement, since many peasants were staunch Roman Catholics while others were followers of Luther or some other religious leader such as Münzer. However, the new teaching, whether of Luther or some other individual, did exert a profound influence which cannot be overlooked. The existence of distortion of doctrine made little difference. For the mass of peasants were illiterate, and what information they received about the new teaching was second-hand and often came as a result of exhortations by fanatics and rabble rousers.

5.

LUTHER AND THE WAR: ACTIONS AND REACTIONS

One of the most interesting aspects of the Peasants' War and one of important significance for Luther and for the future of the Reformation was Luther's own actions and reactions during this revolt. For his anti-peasant position the Reformer has been hotly condemned by many. He has been charged with encouraging the peasants and then discouraging them and even advocating their wholesale slaughter in order to end the conflict. To undertake an objective study one has to examine the three published works which Luther produced during this time and which bear directly on the conflict. It is also necessary, however, to examine some of the letters which Luther wrote as a result of travels throughout the rebellious areas; these also throw some light on Luther's thoughts on rebellion. The three published tracts, which had wide circulation, in chronological order (chronology plays an important part in the analysis) are:

1.   *An Exhortation to Peace Based on the Twelve Articles of the Peasants in Swabia*—April, 1525.

2. *Against the Murderous and Thieving Bands of Peasants* —May, 1525.

3. *An Open Letter Concerning the Harsh Booklet Against the Peasants*—July, 1525.

In March, 1525, at Memmingen, a so-called peasants' parliament assembled and adopted the Twelve Articles. These articles were to be the basis for reform, and were to represent at least in part the program desired by the peasants. It had become quite evident that the peasants were willing to fight and die for these articles. Although it was not the only list of demands drafted by the peasants of Germany,[1] it was the program which directly concerned Martin Luther. The leaders at Memmingen had voiced their willingness, even eagerness, to submit these demands to any competent individual or group of individuals for examination, criticism, and comment. The peasant leaders stated that they would be willing to change any or all of the articles if it could be proved that any were contrary to the Gospel. No formal group met, however, to consider these articles. But Martin Luther, the Wittenberg professor and theologian, did deem it necessary that some reply be given to the peasant program. As a result of this feeling by Luther, he wrote Tract Number One.

This tract, *An Exhortation or Admonition to Peace,*[2] is divided into two main parts: one, an address to the princes; and two, an address to the peasants. In speaking to the princes Luther first repeated some of the same criticisms which he had stated two years earlier in his tract of 1523, *Of Temporal Power, In How Far One Should Obey It.* He criticizes princes, lords, bishops, priests, and monks for their blindness and stupidity, and especially for their vanity. The nobles and clergy as a class live in splendor, and they appear to be flaunting their rich living in the very faces of the poor who are dwelling in want and poverty. How long can one expect the poor to live in this manner and continue to be submissive? The difference in living status between high and low is too great. Luther bluntly states that it is not so much the peasants rising against the nobles as God himself. Luther also takes issue with his critics who claim that he has aided the rebellion by inciting the peasants to riot. The author denies this charge categorically. Everyone who knows Martin Luther and his teaching will admit that he has preached against both sedition and violence and that he has pleaded for obedience even to those nobles whose rule has been the most tyrannical. Luther does not deny that there has been inciting to riot, but it has been by those prophets of murder and violence whom he himself has staunchly fought for three whole years. He then says that if he so wished he could laugh with glee at the present plight of the nobles, but he prays that God may prevent him from doing that.

After this rather bitter criticism of the nobility and clergy Luther turns to the Twelve Articles.[3] He states that some of these demands are so just and fair as to have deprived the nobles of honor and respect in the sight of God. But he, Luther, could have written better articles, such as those which had appeared in the *Address to the German Nobility*. However, since the nobles had not heeded his teaching in 1520, he had not written any new ones. The rulers are now forced to read the peasants' articles. Actually, Luther only discusses the first article concerning the freedom to have the Gospel preached. He considers the peasants justified in their request to hear the preaching of the Gospel. The rulers could not reject this. But he did state that it was unlawful for the peasants to pay their preacher's salary from tithes which legally belong to the government. The preaching of the Gospel cannot be refused by any government. As for the other articles concerning servile dues and similar grievances, these are also just and fair. He admonishes the nobles to seek the welfare of their subjects. The peasants should share with their lords the increases from the fields. The rulers must learn to economize and curtail their spending.

Luther then turns to the peasants. He is more friendly in this section, and he reminds his readers that his own parents also had once been poor people, and he expresses sympathy for these tillers of the soil. It was only after his parents had moved to Mansfeld, where his father was able to acquire a share in some mines, that poverty no longer lived with the Luthers. Although he admits that the lords have been cruel and tyrannical, he admonishes the peasants to remain patient and submissive, and this is the main theme of this entire section. The peasants have no right to make themselves judges to judge the evil deeds of their superiors.

In discussing the Twelve Articles the author states that although a congregation may elect its own pastor, it cannot legally set aside tithes or funds for his support because these tithes legally belong to the government. And if the government refuses to allow this elected pastor to serve his congregation, he should flee to another place, and the congregation may go with him. Tithes are the property of the government, and for the village or community to set aside a part for the pastor and part for the poor is robbery. Luther's discussion of the articles concerning serfdom is rather interesting. Article three says: "Men should be free and not be considered property of another. They do not wish to be free of all authority; that is against God's Will. They want release from Serfdom." Luther rejects this proposition. He says that this article aims at the equality of all human beings, and that it would mean that Christian Liberty consisted of physical relief from temporal burdens. He believes that temporal freedom cannot flourish if all subjects are alike. There have to be some free, some enslaved, some lords, some subjects. The author then refuses to discuss the other articles by saying that they should be referred to competent authorities, since as a preacher of the Gospel he does not have suitable knowledge.

Luther in this tract reveals himself to be a man caught in the middle, and not quite sure of how to extricate himself from this difficult position where he placed himself by writing this tract. No one had asked him to write such a tract. He had decided of his own free choice to make some kind of reply to the Peasants' Twelve Articles. But being in the middle Luther tries to satisfy or at least mollify both sides. He condemns the princes for their vanity and cruelty to the lowly peasant. And he says that the peasant demands are fair and just, particularly in reference to the servile dues and services. Yet in the address to the peasants, he refuses to discuss these articles, saying he is not competent. In other words, a superficial examination seems to indicate that maybe the peasants do have an argument in their favor, but in talking to the peasants when he has to be specific he would rather not commit himself. However, the statement concerning the elected pastor is a clear contradiction. The rulers cannot refuse to have the Gospel preached to the people, but if they elect their own pastor the rulers may forbid him from teaching. Both the pastor and his congregation should flee to another area where they can continue to hear the word of God.

What kind of explanation can be made for Luther? Perhaps, only that he here is trying to be friendly to both sides. He recognizes that there has been cruelty and injustice visited upon many peasants by their lords. And this should be corrected. But he rejects the idea that the peasants can correct this. They have no right to rise against lawfully constituted authority. They must be patient. They must submit to tyranny if that is the case. Evil must be fought and subdued, but not by creating a greater evil in the process. Actually, Luther is making a plea to the rulers on one hand to change their ways, to be good princes and share with their subjects the increased bounty of the fields. On the other, he exhorts the peasants or subjects to be patient and submit to their rulers, arguing that changes will occur, but no force is to be used to bring about these changes.

Almost immediately following the writing and subsequent publication of *An Exhortation to Peace*, Luther made two very important trips which brought him into direct contact with the Peasants' War and with the results of the war in some of the areas devastated by the fighting. Count Albert of Mansfeld had requested that Luther journey to Eisleben, Luther's birthplace, to establish a new Christian school. In the company of Melancthon and Agricola, Luther made the trip. On this visit he was able to gather much information concerning the revolt from people he met and especially from his brother-in-law, John Rühel, the court councillor for the count. With his own eyes he was able to see some of the results of the revolt. Rühel was especially helpful in supplying Luther with information. However, this trip was only the beginning. Although he learned much from the visit to Eisleben, it was not until early May that he ventured forth specifically to view the war, and with the express purpose of preaching against violence and against the war. On this journey, for the first time in his career, Luther met serious opposition from the common people. As a monk and preacher his congregation had always listened with respect and reverence to the famous Dr. Luther. He was honored and respected by his students and fellow faculty members. In 1522 when he returned from the Wartburg with the aim of quelling the disturbances in Wittenberg, he was successful. The people listened and heeded his preaching. In 1525 it was far different. The reception he obtained for example at Nordhausen was not what Martin Luther was expecting. At Nordhausen he was interrupted in the very midst of his sermon by hecklers in the audience.[4] There was no doubt in Luther's mind that the situation was completely out of hand. He could not by his own influence stop the fighting and violence. The situation was too widespread for him to be able to repeat the victory of 1522. Wittenberg was far different from all of southern Germany. He had influence, to be sure, but not enough. On his way home to Wittenberg Luther wrote to Rühel at Mansfeld. The letter indicates clearly what his attitude now was. At Weimar he had stated that he would write another tract. He wrote to Rühel from Seeburg on 4 May 1525:

> They are faithless and perjured, and still worse, they bring the Divine Word and Gospel to shame and dishonor, a most horrible sin. If God in his wrath really lets them accomplish their purpose, for which he has given them no command nor right, we must suffer it as we do other wickedness, but not acquiesce in it as if they did right. . . Look at the government they have set up, the worst that ever was, without order or discipline in it but only pillage. . . Must we indeed acknowledge as our rulers these faithless, perjured, blasphemous robbers, who have no right from God?[5]

Upon his return to Wittenberg on 6 May 1525, Luther immediately began to work on the publication which he had promised during his visit at Weimar. He had set out on this trip with the sole purpose of getting first-hand information concerning the rebellion. His first trip to Eisleben in mid-April was not sufficient to produce the knowledge he needed. His primary concern then had been the establishment of a Christian school. He had to determine for himself, if possible, the extent of the revolt, and to decide if anything could be done by him personally to end this godless struggle. Perhaps, in the back of his mind he was thinking about the Wittenberg disturbances of 1521-1522. He had been successful then in putting an end to the disorders. Maybe he could be successful again. Such was not the case. He soon learned that the disorders of 1525 were far too serious and too widespread for one man's voice to have much influence. With firsthand observation he had seen some of the results of the violence: monasteries and churches looted, castles pillaged, and fields lying untended. And the reports of other observers only confirmed his own fears. These factors coupled with the booing, hissing, and heckling at Nordhausen made up his mind. The heckling must have rung in his ears for a long time. He had to act. It was his duty to take pen and strike out against this godless movement. He had tried to be reasonable and fair. Certainly no one could accuse him of bias on account of the *Exhortation to Peace*. Was it not an example of moderation? But the time for moderation was past. Extreme measures were the only recourse left, and so he wrote his second tract of the Peasants' War, *Against the Murderous and Bobbing Bands of Peasants*.[6] He wanted action. He did not wish to sit quietly and leave the outcome to the Lord as Frederick the Wise desired. No, the only way to treat this mad movement was with the sword.

In this tract Luther reveals a very human weakness: loss of temper and a tendency to use bitter and vituperative language. Perhaps it would have been more expedient for him to have waited for a time after his return from the revolted areas before beginning to write. He might have used this interval to examine more objectively the information which he had gained from his trips and observations. He might have been more calm in his presentation. Luther denounces the peasants with the utmost violence of language, and he urges the government to smite them without pity. He charges that the peasants have broken their oath to the government and as a result are subject to arrest and trial. They had robbed and slain their fellow men and were subject to death in body and soul. And even more heinous, they had attempted to justify their cause and their actions by appealing to Christian Brotherhood. This was blasphemy. No one could justify murder, robbery, and pillage in the name of Christian Brotherhood. For Luther, the latter charge was perhaps the most serious. The peasants were mad dogs which should be slain to protect the people. He speaks to the soldiers of the princes and states that if they die in battle against these murderers, they could never have a more blessed end. It was an honor to suffer injury or even death in this struggle against these evildoers. In order to hinder aid being given to the peasants, material or spiritual, he advises everyone to avoid these peasants just as they do the devil.

Actually Luther expressed nothing new in this tract. He had always denounced revolt against constituted authority. Patience and submission was the main theme of his earlier tract, and the same was true here. But he now saw that the revolt was so serious that only violent measures could be effective in its overthrow. The distinguishing feature of *Against the Murderous and Thieving Bands* was its abusive language, and even this was not too unusual for the sixteenth century when violent and intemperate language was commonplace. The chief criticism of the tract besides its language was its timing. Luther had begun to write on 6 May 1525 after his return. On 15 May 1525, less than two weeks later, the peasants suffered their most disastrous defeat, and what later turned out to be in effect their final defeat at Frankenhausen. This was the crucial battle in the war. Although other battles were fought subsequently, Frankenhausen was the crucial one. The peasant losses were enormous. Münzer was captured and later executed. The backbone of the entire movement was broken. It is not known exactly when the tract was published, but it was probably sometime in May.[7]

This tract was an indictment of the peasants because of their resorting to violence. He was not trying to win popularity with either side. To Luther the peasant movement was a crime against the Government and against God. It must be stopped. He had already tried to appeal to them in a moderate and friendly tone, but had been unsuccessful. The only recourse left was to call upon the government to do its duty.

After this tract was written Luther composed a number of letters in late May which indicate that he had received news of the battle of Frankenhausen. On 25 May he wrote to John Rühel at Mansfeld, in which he inquired specifically about Thomas Münzer. He wanted to have further details of his capture and his conduct. Luther goes on to say that it is pitiful that we have to be so cruel to the poor people, but what can we do? Was there any other recourse than that which was taken? It is necessary and God wills it, so that fear may be brought upon the people. He tells Rühel not to be so worried about this matter since it will profit many souls whom it will terrify and restrain. So there is no doubt that Luther had heard of the capture of Münzer and of the slaughter meted out to the rebels at Frankenhausen. It might have been possible for him at this time, if he so wished, to have recalled from publication his second tract. However, there is no evidence that Luther ever contemplated such an act. His stand was irrevocable. In a letter to Nicholas Amsdorf on 30 May he says that it is better that all the peasants be killed than the magistrates and princes perish because the peasants took the sword without divine authority.[8] The princes, on the other hand, regardless of their tyranny, bear the sword by God's authority. Again in a letter to Rühel[9] Luther touches on the question of mercy for the peasants, a question which had been asked many times since the princes started to become victorious. His reply to these pleas is that if the peasants are innocent then God will save and protect them. If he does not protect them, then they are certainly not innocent, but have at least kept silent and approved the rebellion. If they did nothing because of fear, it is a sin in the sight of God like the man who denies Christ because he is afraid. "We ought to pray for them that they may be obedient; if not, then let the shot whistle, or they will make things a thousandfold worse." Thus to Martin Luther there were only two sides to this revolt; the side of the princes and that of the rebels. There was no middle ground. There was no room for neutrality, and those people that did nothing, either to aid or hinder the peasant movement, were as guilty as the rebels for their acquiescence. It seemed to Luther that this was a sign of their approval of the peasant movement. He placed the entire blame on the peasants and their leaders.

Ever since the publication of his second tract concerning the Peasants' War Luther had been urged by friends and supporters to write a further explanation of his stand and perhaps lessen the shock which the second tract had produced. After his marriage to Katie Luther, he considered these urgings, and decided to issue one more tract on the subject. By July 1525, when the third tract appeared, the war for practical purposes was ended. It is true that pockets of resistance still remained, and that there was even fighting in Luther's own native Thuringia. But he knew that the backbone of the revolt had been broken. The princes and nobility were surely if slowly wiping out the rebel forces. It was only a matter of time. But time to Luther was important. The fighting should cease immediately. As long as the revolt continued, it needed the strongest measures possible to stop it. And so Luther wrote *A Letter Concerning the Harsh Booklet Against the Peasants*.[10] If anyone was of the belief that Luther was going to change his views expressed in tract number two or to soften the language or opinions expressed, that person was badly mistaken. "As I wrote in my treatise against the peasants, so I write now. Let no one take pity on the hardened, obstinate, and blinded peasants who will not listen; let anyone who can and is able hew down, stab, and slay them as one would a mad dog. An ass must be beaten and rabble governed by force. The intention of the devil was to lay Germany waste, because he was unable to prevent in any other way the spread of the Gospel." Some of his critics had stated that Luther showed no mercy toward the rebels when they were being defeated. He had advocated beating a fallen man. In his third tract Luther takes up the problem of mercy. He says that in the Kingdom of the World —and he clearly distinguishes between the Kingdom of God and the Kingdom of the World—the government cannot exercise mercy but must punish with the sword. He goes on to say how much better everything would have been for all Germany if the authorities had promptly and expeditiously punished the first one hundred peasants. Thousands would have been saved from death and injury. But this was not done. As a result, all of Germany had gone up in flames. The peasants had had a harsh lesson to learn, but it was the will of God. The nobles also had a lesson to learn, and it was that they should realize how to treat their peasants as they deserved to be treated. They should have punished them when they needed it and not have waited until the situation was out of hand.

In examining the three published tracts pertaining to the Peasants' War as well as the related letters which the reformer had written to friends and associates, we can clearly see that two main themes are present, and that at no time did Luther ever deviate from this line of thought. One, the people should be patient and submissive to their rulers, and under no circumstances resort to violence to curb evil. The princes rule by divine right and rebellion against such authority is against the will of God, and as such an act of the devil. Two, the princes and nobles should rule their subjects with justice, and should share with their peasants the abundance which God had granted to them. They should put aside vanity which had been one of the prime causes of the revolt. They should learn to economize and live simply. During the revolt these themes were first enunciated in the *Exhortation to Peace*, and although Luther did use violent and savage language in his two later tracts, the fact remains that he did not change his basic views. Whereas the first was in reality an exhortation to stop the fighting, the latter two were severe indictments of the peasant movement and its leaders in which charges were presented and a sentence was recommended. In reality Luther considered the peasants guilty of one of the most heinous crimes which he could imagine: the attempt to overthrow their legal rulers.

Some of his critics have claimed that he was conciliatory in the first tract, and so damning in the others. Perhaps mediation was his aim. He urged both sides to present their grievances for study. Arbitration and mediation was the method to settle differences, not force. He had stated forthrightly that the princes in many cases were both cruel and tyrannical, and that they had brought this revolt upon themselves by their very actions. But he had also argued that the peasants must not resort to violence to change their conditions since this would be creating a greater evil than that which they wanted to destroy. There is no basic inconsistency present in these writings. Perhaps, there are contradictions in detail, but not in basic tenets. It must be remembered that Luther was at times headstrong and hot tempered. The two later tracts do not show a cool head necessarily, for Luther was both angry and afraid. He was angry at the revolt against legally constituted government; and, he was afraid of its effect on his teaching and his movement. The peasant leaders had disgraced the Gospel. They had distorted Luther's teachings to suit their own selfish purposes. He considered that they had dishonored the very name of Christ. How could any one justify their demands for release from serfdom or demand equality of all men by an appeal to the Gospel or by citing the words of Dr. Martin Luther?

Luther was also afraid for personal reasons. This is not meant to imply physical cowardice by any means. After his trip through the revolting areas when he had seen some of the devastation, and when he personally had experienced the shock of being heckled by the common man, what would the town of Wittenberg and the Black Cloister for example expect if the rebellion was successful?

During the past few decades a large number of German and American historians have presented Luther as reactionary, as well as superstitious; and they have given Münzer a much larger role in the movement than heretofore. Perhaps the most distinguished of these are Professor Roland H. Bainton of Yale University and Heinz Kamnitzer of Humbolt University in Berlin. The latter's work is more recent and more important.[11] In his

book on the origins of the Peasants' War, he devotes an entire
section to Münzer. He argues that Münzer gradually surpassed
Luther as a popular leader, and regards him as the greatest
figure in the Reformation. This is contrary to all previous interpretations, and is based largely on the work of Friedrich Engels.
The latter strongly urges the reader to study a Marxist interpretation presented in M. M. Smirin, *Die Volksreformation des
Thomas Münzer und der grosze Bauernkrieg* (Berlin, 1952).
According to Smirin, there were four theses by Münzer which
were of great significance: (1) The Kingdom of God on earth
would be made possible through the liberation of the lower
classes in the social and economic order. (2) In the cities and
rural territories, laborers must have justice done to them. (3)
The German system of government must be eliminated and re-
placed by communal organizations. Castles and monasteries must
be destroyed, and a central government must take the place of
the former princes and municipal councils. (4) The new order
must be based upon the precepts contained in the Holy Scriptures
(Bible).

From these arguments by Münzer, we must derive the opinion

Bainton argues that there would have been no Peasants' War
in Saxony without Thomas Münzer. Since serfdom had been
abolished in Saxony, there was little demand for social and economic reform. Münzer was the only person in his generation who
observed that faith did not accompany physical exhaustion. He
opposed Luther's thesis that the poor people had enough in their
faith, when in fact usury and taxes impede the generation of
faith. Luther claimed that the Bible was sufficient, but the average person was so busy making a living that he had no time
to read the Bible. The princes fleeced their subjects with usury
and by prohibiting them from making use of the fish in the
streams, the birds in the air, and the grass in the fields. Luther
wrongly supported the princes here. He was the Pope at Wittenberg. Luther was against rebellion, but he must have known
that the sword belonged to the whole community.[12]

From these arguments by Münzer, we must derive the opinion
that he was very much interested in material possessions on the

part of his followers; certainly more so than Luther was. The latter often argued that if a person could not worship as he pleased in his country, he should leave it to find a better place. That would involve economic sacrifices, which in Luther's view were of less importance than the loss of religious freedom. Münzer was obviously attracted by the primitive form of society among the early Christians in Jerusalem, as it was described in the Acts of the Apostles, in the New Testament. Here was a form of communism, and this was literally duplicated by the Anabaptist rulers of Münster in the year 1535. Luther was very much opposed to the Anabaptists, as was Calvin. Professor Bainton, *also*, argues that Münzer alone, of all the early Protestants, understood the dependence of saving faith upon material welfare.

Professor Kamnitzer, by publishing in 1952 the intriguing work by Alfred Meusel on the Peasants' War, and by issuing his own book on that subject in 1953, showed that in Germany, as well as in Russia, the idea is gaining ground of a Luther who was acting as a veritable Pope among his followers. Even in the United States during the year 1958 there were orthodox Calvinists who joined the revisionists. Says Professor Kamnitzer: "A. Meusel was the first to call attention to the following facts: Luther threatened the princes with a serious revolt on the part of the left wing of the Protestant Reformation if the secular authorities did not support his own cause, which was that of the upper bourgeoisie. The princes had better defend his moderate program of reformation, as he had announced it in his suppression of the radical movement inaugurated at Wittenberg by Karlstadt and his followers."[13] The latter gleefully confiscated an enormous amount of eccelesiastical property. Luther was very successful with his pamphlet, *A True Warning to all Christians to Beware of Rebellion and Uprising*. The plebeians must not be permitted to run wild and upset things for the princes and property owners, of whom Luther was a good representative when, upon his marriage in June, 1525, he received as a wedding gift the whole monastery from the new elector of Saxony. That was, however, three years after the pamphlet in question was published by Luther.

6.

SOME ECONOMIC ASPECTS OF LUTHER'S POSITION DURING THE PEASANTS' WAR

In considering the role that Martin Luther played during the Great Peasants' War, it is necessary to examine in some detail Luther's own economic position in 16th century Saxony. This approach necessitates a threefold examination of economic factors: one, the social and economic position of the Luther family with particular emphasis on Hans Luther, Martin's father; two, Luther's own economic status in Wittenberg as a faculty member and as the leader of a new movement; and three, a brief examination of Luther's own economic ideas as found in his written tracts devoted to economic problems.[1]

Early biographers and students of the life of the Great Reformer, whether Roman Catholic or Protestant, emphasized greatly Luther's peasant background. This emphasis was especially important for his supporters to show Luther's sympathy for and close ties with the common people. And of course, they tried to show that being of peasant background, he knew the peasants and their problems and was in complete sympathy with them. Only the means of dealing with these problems varied. His opponents, using this same argument, attempted to prove that Luther had turned his back on his ancestors, and that during the war, instead of supporting them, he vilified them, and condemned them to death. He was thus a traitor to his own ancestral heritage.

It is very unfortunate for the student of Luther that the man left no autobiography; nor did any of his close associates such as Philip Melanchthon, take it upon themselves to write a comprehensive biography of their leader. Melanchthon did write a brief sketch amounting to about ten pages on the life of Luther, but this is far from an adequate coverage. And this is particularly true where the early life or childhood of Luther is concerned. The Table Talks do contain various references to his childhood, but it must be remembered that these reports vary greatly, depending on the authors, and that even Luther himself was apt to exaggerate or to gloss over events of his youth.

The family name, Luther, as we know it today, had a variety of spellings—Ludher, Luder, Lueder, Luther, and Lauter.[2] The ancestral home of the Luther family seems to have been in the Moehra region, southwest of the Thurginian Forest in the neighborhood of Eisenach. It is interesting to note that the Luthers belonged to a group known as the *Erbzinsleute*. This term designated a family grouping holding a village and surrounding territory in a kind of communal ownership. However, it is extremely important to mention that the family members were not serfs. They were free individuals. The *Zins* or tax which was owed to the Elector and to the church was a tax on the land, and was not a head tax. Thus the Luthers were not serfs in the sense of owing various dues and services to a local lord. They were small landed properties whose legal obligation was to pay a tax both to the church and to the elector of Saxony. They were free individuals.

The family grouping obeyed the custom that the estate was inherited by the youngest son, not the eldest, and it was for this reason that Hans Luther, Martin's father, left the family domains to strike out on his own. This too was the usual custom. The eldest son, as a rule, left the home and migrated to another part of Saxony to secure his fortune in new lands, and to build up an estate of his own. This system was fortunate at least in that it avoided the pitfalls of continuous divisions of the inheritance among all sons, until the divisions were so small that no living could be had from the land. It can be assumed that the Luther family, as was true of others throughout the passing generations, had increased greatly in numbers. In 1521, when Luther stopped at Moehra on his way to Worms, he learned that his people occupied the whole region between Eisenach and Rennsteig. It was not usually necessary for the elder sons to move very far. Actually, then, the region encompassed by the Luthers was not necessarily large. These were people with a strong affinity for the soil.

In the area of western Thuringia, not far from the Wartburg, Hans Luther was born, reared, and married. Hans was the eldest of four sons, of Heine Luder and Margarethe Lindemann, and was known in his family as Gross-Hans. Gross-Hans married Margarethe Ziegler, a young woman of the neighborhood. Shortly after the marriage, the young couple moved to Eisleben, as the eldest son Hans knew that he could not inherit any part of the family estate. Eisleben seemed a promising location since the mining industry (copper) was at this time a flourishing enterprise. The young couple moved into a two-story house in the southeastern section of the city. The very fact that the home of Luther's birth was a multistory dwelling has important significance since few peasants of the time could possibly have afforded to live in such a structure. In the summer of 1484, when Martin Luther was less than a year old, the family moved to Mansfeld. The reasons for the move were probably economic, although no conclusive reasons can be given. However, Hans was an ambitious young man, and it is quite feasible that Mansfeld, closer to the Harz Mountains, and more in the heart of the mining industry, held out a better economic future for the young man and his new family than did Eisleben.

The fact that Hans and Margarethe were poor at this time cannot be denied. They were just getting started and had just moved to a new location in the hopes of bettering their financial position. Poverty was no crime, and this could be remedied in time. The familly of Hans Luther were burghers and were quite separate from the lowly peasant who played such an important part in the war of 1524-25. Hans quickly bettered his position in Mansfeld, and in 1491 when Martin was only eight years old, Hans Luther was made a burgher to protect the rights of his fellow citizens in the city council.[3] Certainly the character of Hans Luther was an important factor in his selection. This was an important position, and one which would be given only to a man of substance and one respected by his fellow burghers. One cannot overlook the possible financial implications of such a choice. The Luthers were by now a steadily rising young couple who were making something of themselves. They had started from the bottom so to speak, but with thrift and hard work they had reached a position where Hans could be selected to protect the rights of all citizens in the council. The virtues of thrift and hard work must indeed have played a great part in his selection, but so must his economic position. He had gone far in the eight years since his arrival in the town. How Hans Luther became a mine operator for himself is not known. It is known, for example, that in 1507 Hans renewed a five-year lease on a mine, so he must have been an operator since 1502. Perhaps, it would not be stretching the point too much if one said that by the beginning of the 16th century Hans Luther was in business for himself, and as a self-employed businessman, he operated either by lease or outright ownership both mines and furnaces. It is not known how many men he employed. Undoubtedly the mines were small, and so not many men were needed.

In Mansfeld, Hans and Margarthe Luther were able to purchase a home, and could afford to educate their eldest son, Martin, in a manner no mere peasant lad could hope to receive. In fact, when Luther matriculated at the University of Erfurt, the records classified him as being from a family that "had."[4]

When Martin became a priest, Hans Luther visited the monastery with a company of 20 horsemen and gave a gift of 20 gulden to the Augustinians. This was considered a rather handsome gift since the price of an ox at the time was usually one or two gulden. It is estimated that Hans left an estate of approximately $18,000. This was equivalent to $250,000 in our value. It is correct that the Luthers were far from simple peasants.

The above brief description of Luther's family in economic matters is not meant by any means as an attempt to disqualify Luther as a friend of the common man, nor is it an attempt to prove that Luther was not and could not be sympathetic with the people who worked the soil. If one uses the term peasant and farmer to mean any person who farmed, whether he owned his land or not, then perhaps Luther's ancestors can be called peasants. But a distinction must be made between peasant and farmer.

A peasant can be considered anyone who tilled the land, but did not own it; a farmer was one who tilled his *own* land. It is inconceivable that a lowly peasant of the type who took part in the revolt could have accumulated the wealth that Hans Luther did. Nor could a mere peasant have sent his son to such a succession of schools: Mansfeld, Magdeburg, Eisenach, and the University of Erfurt. No, Luther's family were not peasants. Martin's grandfather was a farmer. His own father, only a few years after his birth, was a respected and financially sound burgher in Mansfeld. They were not wealthy in the sense of the Fuggers by any means. But they were free individuals, and were members of the new but rising middle class. It was still somewhat early in Saxony to consider a separate and distinct class, neither nobles nor clergy, as having significant influence in political affairs. But there was at least a nucleus of this middle class (certainly in economic matters) and the Luthers were certainly members of it. Therefore it is erroneous to say that Martin Luther turned his back on his own people, the peasants, and asked the lords to kill them. Nor can he be condemned as having lost touch with these people since he never was a peasant.[5]

The second part of Luther's economic life which has to be examined is Luther's own economic wealth and position in 16th century Wittenberg. It has been shown above how Luther's own family were fairly well-to-do burghers of Mansfeld. Originally they had been farmers, but through ambition, hard work, intelligence, and careful planning Hans Luther had become a mine operator in the copper region and the family had acquired a reputation as being a family that "had." Thus Luther had this as a background when he joined the Augustinians. He had never had any real experience with poverty or want. What he knew of such things was learned from the talk of his parents about their early life in the Moehra region and in Eisleben and Mansfeld. However, Martin had been too young to remember any hardships which the family might have endured. He was only eight years old when his father was selected as a representative to the town council. The family was not yet wealthy. Martin's mother gathered wood for herself. No household in Mansfeld was without hard manual labor, and the woman of the house had much hard work to perform. Unless the family were members of the upper nobility or there was considerable wealth, all family members had to work hard. This background then of a well-to-do burgher family, financially prosperous and socially accepted and respected, was of vital importance in understanding Luther's position in 1524 and 1525.

Up to the time of the final break with Rome, Luther was a monk who had given up any personal financial gains and personal fortune. None was needed. However, once the break with Rome became a fact and Luther renounced monasticism together with monks and other members of the clergy who got married, then personal finances necessarily became important. It is only at this time that the personal finances of Martin Luther can be considered.

There are three main factors which must be weighed in evaluating the personal economic position of the Reformer: (1) his income as a professor of theology on the faculty of the University of Wittenberg; (2) income from his numerous publications, plus gifts from Frederick the Wise and the other nobles sympathetic to Luther's cause; and (3) property in the form of real estate which either was purchased by Luther or was given to him. It should be remembered, however, that land was still the most important basis for wealth in 16th-century Germany.

Unfortunately no figures on faculty salaries exist for the early years of the University of Wittenberg. However, due to the reorganization in 1536, figures are available which will have to be used even though this date is much later than the Peasants' War. As a professor of theology, Luther's salary came to the equivalent of about $4,000 per year. This seems little enough and certainly one could not become wealthy on such an income. But it was a reasonably good income for the time, and there were certain compensations involved. Faculty members were exempt from all but extraordinary taxes. Also there were certain fees from students which were paid directly to the professor. In effect, Luther lived modestly but well. There is no evidence anywhere that Martin ever had to skimp or do without necessities. He was adequately provided with funds. And whenever it became evident that the annual salary would not stretch throughout the whole year, the elector always made provisions for additional income to his reformer. Naturally, Katie had a lot to do with how far the salary did go. She was a frugal woman who at times must have become annoyed with Luther's openhandedness. The Luther table was always filled with guests including fellow professors and students.[6] There were few meals when someone other than the family was not present. However, no great emphasis should be placed on Luther's income as a professor other than to say that it provided him with an adequate living. He could be comfortable and relatively free from financial worry.

Income from publications such as tracts and his German Bible was negligible. Luther wanted as wide a circulation as possible so that his ideas could be read by as many people as possible. Thus the price of the pamphlet as a rule covered no more than the price of publication. However, it was the practice to send copies to court and other influential and wealthy people. Gifts usually followed. And these at times were not inconsiderable. Actually, the bulk of Luther's wealth consisted of gifts. His income as a professor was usually spent before the end of the fiscal year, and he had to rely on gifts from the elector for the remaining time. Perhaps a brief list of Luther's possessions would help to illustrate the financial holdings of the Great Reformer:

1. Zulsdorf property with improvements	$ 8,174
2. Books and jewels	13,400
3. Black Cloister	80,400
4. Brauer Haus	5,628
5. Wolf's Garden	268
6. Garden on the Swine Market	5,628
7. Small farm and garden	1,206
8. 5 cows	201
9. 9 large calves	241
10. A goat with two kids	27
11. 8 pigs	107
12. 2 sows	167
13. 3 little pigs	13
14. 50 *adde* (florins)	670[7]

It is evident that real estate comprised the bulk of Luther's wealth, and knowing that the largest item, the Black Cloister, was a gift by the elector to Luther as a wedding present, it can be said that the bulk of his fortune came from gifts. Luther's income from his salary and publications was by no means adequate to purchase such large holdings of property. And his property was valuable. What he had comprised a well-planned economic unit. A family need for shelter and food was well provided by the above list. Undoubtedly Katie made few purchases at the local store.

It was shown in presenting the Twelve Articles of the Peasants of Swabia that economic demands were predominant. The increased importance of trade in the European economy was playing havoc with the peasant class. Therefore, it is necessary to examine, albeit briefly, some of Luther's attitudes, ideas, and theories on economic problems.[8]

First of all it should be stressed rather strongly that Martin Luther was not primarily interested in economic matters. Luther was a theologian, and was the acknowledged leader of a new movement. His disinterest in economic matters is well illustrated by Professor Hyma, who has written that Luther devoted only about one hundred folio pages to economic questions out of a total of approximately forty thousand.[9] Nevertheless, as the leader of a growing movement which was assuming vast social implications, Luther could not remain blind to economic questions. He had to make certain pronouncements and to publish articles on these matters. Even though he knew and admitted that he was not an authority on such matters, yet he did not recognize any other human being as an authority either. The final authority rested in the Word of God. It was not necessary to examine the writings of past or present authors. All answers relating to economic questions could be found in the Bible. He, Luther, could find the answers himself.

In discussing Luther's attitudes toward the economic problems of his day it is necessary to break down this topic into three main divisions for clarity. They are: (1) Luther's pronouncements relating to interest and usury; (2) his general attitudes toward commerce and the importance of agriculture in the

European economy; and (3) the role of the government in the economy, plus taxation.

The bulk of the one hundred pages devoted to economics may be found in three tracts which the reformer wrote prior to the outbreak of the Peasants' War. This is not to mean that he made no other comments. But these three tracts contain his attitudes toward economic questions. These are: *Short Sermon on Usury* (1519); *Long Sermon on Usury* (1520), and *On Trade and Usury* (1524). After 1524, although he discussed these same problems, he added nothing new to what he had already said.

Usurious rates of interest were far too common in Luther's times not to elicit some kind of attack by a man of Luther's character. Something had to be done about this evil practice where rates of twenty percent and even higher, sometimes reaching one hundred percent, were charged to borrowers. He considered such practices a form of theft that should be stamped out with all possible speed. Very briefly it can be said that he favored a fluctuating rate of interest, but at no time should the rate ever exceed about ten percent. The rate should be determined by the general economic conditions prevailing at the time. If a farmer borrowed a sum at X percent interest, and then the farmer due to bad weather had a very poor crop yield, then that farmer should not have to pay any interest for that year. Actually, Luther favored no interest where possible. This was the act of a real Christian. This perhaps sounds naive since the creditor would be denying himself revenue from capital which he could have invested elsewhere. Luther favored loans where real estate was the security, and from this point of view he never deviated. Although he wrote many times about interest, and each time seemingly from a different angle, yet this one fact remained constant. Luther actually favored no interest at all, as the Jews practised among themselves. But he was aware of the fact that the practice of taking interest was well established, and that the church had been a practitioner of this for many years. He could do nothing to stamp it out, but he might be able to mitigate some of the abuses. In fact, Luther justified the taking of interest in two specific cases, and once more his consistency is revealed: (1) interest on loans where real estate was the security; and (2)

interest determined by the situation of the creditor. If the creditor
was moderately rich and had been receiving interest for some
time, the debtor should receive a reduction in rate. If, on the
other hand, the creditor was aged and poor, the interest rate
should continue unchanged. Luther favored a flexible rate of
interest, varying with general economic conditions. However,
he seems to have favored five percent, and in some cases even
six, seven, or eight percent.

Now let us turn to Luther's attitude toward commerce and
agriculture. Luther's Saxony was over 90 percent agricultural, and
it was only natural that he should have favored agricultural pursuits. He was not completely opposed to trade and commerce,
but he did feel that commerce generally had brought little good
to the people. One of Luther's chief criticisms of the clergy and of
the nobility had been their almost complete preoccupation with
worldly pomp and splendor. The desire for luxuries was an evil,
and part of this was caused by the trade and commerce which
was bringing newer and more expensive goods into Germany.
There was too much emphasis on material possessions. He felt
that Germany produced enough to satisfy the wants of her
people. Why import silks and velvet when Germany produced
large quantities of flax, wool, and hair? Spices too were super-
fluous. Luther felt that commerce should be reduced, and that
agriculture should be increased proportionately.

The last point in Luther's approach to economic questions of
the day was the role which he felt the government should assume
in the economic life of the state. Actually, Luther had very little
to say about the role of the government in economic affairs.
However, he did mention at various times the possible role which
the government might play. In his tract of 1524, *On Trade and
Usury*, Luther listed a number of abuses which were in existence
in Germany at the time. Among these abuses was the attempt by
some unscrupulous businessmen to exhort too high prices for
their wares. Luther then suggested that the government regulate
prices when expedient, but he hoped that such action would not
be necessary.[10] In other words, government intervention should
be undertaken only as a last resort. He was not recommending
such action for everyday use. He even set up a type of measure-

ment for a so-called fair price. The average wage earned by a laborer should be set as a standard, and then using this as a basis and considering the energy, ability, and industry of the businessman, a fair price could be computed.

Luther's second pronouncement concerning government in economic affairs was rather indirect since it did not involve government action, but was in reality a comment on taxes which should be paid to the government. There was no monarch in 16th-century Europe who did not have a severe financial problem. Even within the empire the penny tax had failed so that there was actually no set tax revenue for the government unless in cases of special emergencies such as the Turkish wars. Luther's approach was typically Biblical. He looked to the example set by Joseph in Egypt and Moses and the Children of Israel. Every individual was to turn over to the state a certain percentage of his property or income. The rate was indefinite. The Children of Israel had set aside one-tenth; Joseph had established one-fifth. The rate would vary depending on economic conditions.

In summing up Luther's attitudes toward current economic problems of his times, care must be taken not to endow the Reformer with too many advanced economic theories. The field of economic thought was somewhat strange to Luther. He was a theologian and not an economic expert. If his views seemed conservative, liberal, or radical, he himself admitted, and quite readily, that he was not an authority on such matters, and even though he did not recognize any one else as an authority, this does not detract from his straightforward statement.

The most important aspects in the economic life of Martin Luther, therefore, involve three points: (1) Martin Luther had come from a family that was fairly well-to-do financially. The father was a mine operator and had been elected as a representative on the town council to represent his fellow citizens. Martin's father was able to give his eldest son an education of the highest order, and one which was by no means inexpensive. Possibly it can be said that such a succession of schools which Martin attended could only have happened to a young student whose family had some reasonable economic means. (2) As a faculty member and as a leader of the new reform movement

Luther had accumulated a rather large estate for himself, something which would undoubtedly have pleased his thrifty parents. Luther was not wealthy, but he certainly was not a poor man either. He was a man of property with considerable holdings in real estate. His annual income although not large was augmented by rather substantial gifts from his royal and wealthy supporters. At no time was the Reformer and his own immediate family ever threatened by scarcity of the esentials of life. (3) Luther was a man who was gravely concerned about the economic life of the the people and particularly of the people of Germany. He was witness to the lavish living of the papal court and of some of the members of the higher nobility. He was aware of the importance which these people placed on luxuries, and this was spreading to other people too who should be more watchful over their spiritual needs rather than their material ones. He was witnessing the rapid growth in trade and commerce, and he himself could see little good in all this. Saxony was agricultural; it produced enough for all its inhabitants. Why should people devote so much of their energy and income to this seeking after luxuries?

These three points merely have brought out the fact that Martin Luther was no different from many of his contemporaries. His economic ideas were not revolutionary nor was his economic position in Wittenberg so far different from others around him. True, as the central figure in the reform movement and as a most prolific writer, he probably received more gifts than others. But these factors alone do not set him apart. The disturbing events of the Peasants' War did however highlight these economic factors. The big question to be answered in view of Luther's economic status and in view of his solutions to the current economic problems was what would Luther have gained from a winning peasantry? The peasants lost, and as was shown in Chapter Four, the position of the peasants for the most part worsened as a result of their defeat. But what if they had been victorious? How would Martin Luther, the man of substance, have fared under such conditions? He had visited the revolted areas, and had seen with his own eyes some of the results of a winning peasantry. Monasteries, churches, whole villages, and fields all destroyed. The results were shocking. If we leave aside for the time being any consideration of the possible effect on his movement and ignore for the time being his political beliefs, it is possible that Luther had cause to fear that people in his economic position would lose everything. The burgher class was in the middle. He might sympathize with the poor conditions of the peasants, and he had lashed out against the abuses which nobles were visiting upon their people. Would the city of Wittenberg, the center of the reform movement, be spared from the ravages which had occurred elsewhere? Possibly. But even if it were, what was to happen to people like Luther's own parents? They were substantial citizens of Mansfeld. Could any guarantee be given during a revolt? This was not just a war; it was a revolt of the poorer citizens against the oppression of the rich. There seems little likelihood that any such guarantee could be given. Certainly the reformer's property would be respected. But in the heat of battle, and more likely in the joy of victory, much would be destroyed, and looting would be rampant. It was true that in 1525 Luther was just beginning to acquire a considerable estate. It was only in June when he married Katie that he received the most valuable of his gifts, the Black Cloister.

It is necessary to consider that economic considerations did play a part in Luther's determination to do everything in his power to see the peasants' illegal acts and plans defeated. Perhaps, economic factors can be considered by some to be inconsequential. The weight assigned to them will vary with the individual. Regardless, they must be considered in any evaluation of Luther's role in the war.

7.

LUTHER'S POLITICS: PART ONE

Before examining in further detail the political ideas and theories of Martin Luther, it is necessary first to look at the political situation in the Holy Roman Empire during the time of

Luther himself. He was a subject of Frederick the Wise, one of the seven electors of the empire. The office of emperor was elective, although since the 15th century the title of emperor was held only by members of the Hapsburg family. But the great power of this family did not detract from the elective principle and from the powers of the various electors. It had been the practice of the candidates, whether they be Hapsburgs or not, to grant concessions in the form of capitulations to the territorial princes of the empire in order to gain support for their candidacy. These capitulations had the result of depriving the emperor, once elected, of many powers, and of placing more and more authority in the hands of the territorial princes including the electors. Actually the office of Holy Roman Emperor contained little real political power. The emperors were strong territorial princes; their authority was based almost exclusively on their position as dukes of Austria and as hereditary lords within the Austrian lands themselves. As emperor, the highest lord in the empire did not have a regular imperial revenue to sustain him and his empire, nor did he have a regularly constituted army for the defense of the empire. On the contrary, the emperor was forced to rely on the good faith and loyalty of the various territorial princes within the empire to support him and his policies. In the imperial election of 1519, Charles I of Spain was chosen as the new emperor with the title of Charles V. It was at this time that the Hapsburgs became the most powerful noble family in Europe. Charles brought with him into the Hapsburg domains both Spain and the Netherlands, and although Spain was not considered a part of the Holy Roman Empire, it contributed to the consolidation of the Hapsburg domains under one head. And the territories that were included in the empire were to influence and color the policies of Charles V. He became more interested with his position as head of the House of Hapsburg with its wide holdings, than as head of the Empire with only nominal authority and power.

Yet Charles called himself Emperor of the Romans and Augustus Forever, besides King of Germany, Hungary, Dalmatia, etc., as well as ruler of the Indies, both islands and the mainland,

meaning America plus the Malay Archipelago. When Luther
stood before such a person, many spectators were struck with
awe. But the seven electors had their own opinions about the
claims made by their emperor. At the Diet of Worms they took
care that Ferdinand of Hapsburg, the younger brother of Charles,
should rule Austria, Hungary, Tyrol, Croatia, and Dalmatia, thus
keeping Charles out of business as far as the German-speaking
countries were concerned. And as for the Duchy of Burgundy,
that was taken by the King of France from Mary of Burgundy
upon her father's death in 1477. Although Charles V enjoyed his
title, Duke of Burgundy, he was not its ruler. The same may be
said about Jerusalem, which remained firmly in the hands of the
Turks. Nevertheless, such was his prestige that Pope Clement VII
in 1529 did not dare to grant to King Henry VIII of England a
divorce from Catherine of Aragon, aunt of Charles V. The head of
the Roman Catholic Church had reason for fearing Charles, for
the Pope had recently spent several months as prisoner in a
famous building near the Vatican Palace in Rome. There he had
been surrounded by soldiers from the Holy Roman Empire employed by Charles, who as King of Naples and Sicily, and Duke
of Milan, had much to say about ecclesiastical affairs in Italy and
Spain.

The Empire in fact was a conglomeration of principalities,
varying in size from the great duchies down to the small but by
no means insignificant Free Cities. The various units of the empire vied with each other for power and vied also with the emperor himself. When it came time for an election, the candidates
would grant concessions to the various units in order to gain votes
and support.

The Holy Roman Empire was split not only politically into
many different and often antagonistic units, it was also split on
a very important religious-political matter. This was the struggle
between the ecclesiastical and secular authorities. In its long fight
for domination in the western church, the papacy had put forward
many propositions leading to the papal pretension of final authority over the secular rulers. The emperor was to be crowned by the
Pope; kings were to be crowned by Bishops; the other territorial

lords, dukes, counts, and so forth, were to receive the symbols of their respective office from the appropriate ecclesiastical official. The papacy was claiming that it was above emperor and kings. And the church led by the papal party even claimed the audacious right of being able to depose secular rulers.

This extreme papal position was strongly opposed by many of the early Holy Roman Emperors. The figures of Henry IV and Frederick II are only two who vigorously and avidly fought against papal pretensions in the political sphere. Even by the 16th century the question of who was supreme had not been fully answered. There remained within the Roman Catholic Church strong proponents of papal supremacy. And it must be remembered that there were protagonists among the secular lords themselves. This problem had caused bitter conflicts in the past, as in the case of the two emperors already named. And this conflict of interest among the temporal authorities, princes, counts, and dukes, within the empire, and the extreme papal party was still in existence during the life of Martin Luther. The conflict in Western Europe was to be further complicated by the rise of the national monarchies, particularly in France, England, and Spain. The struggle was to be partially resolved as a result of the Reformation itself. But even in such states as France and Spain, where Roman Catholicism remained the religion of most people and even the State Religion, the state would continue to vie with the extreme papal party for ultimate control of secular affairs, and the secular authority was to win in many cases over the ardent Romanists, as Luther termed them.[1]

Although Martin Luther was trained as a theologian, and of course was primarily concerned with theological matters, surprisingly enough he wrote prodigiously on matters far removed from theology. His economic ideas and social status have already been discussed. His output on political matters was far greater than on economics. One should not be too surprised at the long list of writings which Luther devoted to politics, since political developments were a vital issue to this leader of a new movement. And even before he had been condemned at Worms, he wrote perhaps his most important political treatises.

In examining Luther's political writings, whether these be in tracts devoted exclusively to politics or whether they be mere references in tracts and letters to other problems, there are three main points which Luther discussed, and which shall be examined in detail. The first of these is the Separation of Church and State. As explained above, this was an important political question of the time, and it had been for several centuries in western Europe. Luther had very definite ideas and thoughts on the powers of the State in relation to the Church. The second topic which Luther discusses concerns the limitations of Secular Authority, and how citizens or subjects should act in the face of unjust or tyrannical rulers. In other words, what rights do subjects have to change the order of things or to change the policies of rulers within a state? The third deals with Luther's concepts of the ideal government. What government did Luther advocate if any? And also what should good rulers do and what are the requisites for good government and for good rulers? These three main points are found repeatedly expressed and discussed in Luther's works concerning political matters. However, it should be pointed out that the time limit of 1525 is being set as a general rule, since these three main points and the bulk of writings on politics occur before and during the year 1525. It will be seen that his political beliefs were actually far advanced before the outbreak of activities in 1524 which led up to the war. And the decided consistency in Luther's attitude and ideas toward government will be found.[2]

The clearest exposition of Luther's ideas on Church and State is found in the famous and thunderous tract *An Open Letter to the Christian Nobility of the German Nation Concerning Reform of the Christian Estate*.[3] This tract is divided into three main parts:

1. The Three Walls of the Romanists.
2. Abuses to be discussed in Councils.
3. Proposals for Reform.

Only Parts One and Three need concern us at this time. In Part One Luther claimed that the ardent papal party, the Romanists, had built three walls about them which prevented reform and which had caused terrible corruption throughout all Christendom. He then proceeded to tear down these walls by argument. These three walls were:

1. When pressed by temporal power, the Romanists issued decrees and said that temporal power had no jurisdiction over them.

2. When attempts were made to reprove these Romanists by Scripture, they said that interpretations of the Scripture belonged only to the Pope.

3. If threatened by a council, they said that only the Pope could call a council.

It was the attack on the first of these three walls which concern us. It clearly showed Luther's position regarding the powers of the Church in relation to the State and vice versa. The attack on the first wall was quite vehement:

> It is pure invention that Pope, bishops, priests and monks are to be called the "Spiritual estate!" That is indeed a fine bit of lying and hypocrisy. Yet no one should be frightened by it; and for this reason—viz., that all Christians are truly of the "spiritual estate," and there is among them no difference at all but that of office, as Paul says in I Corinthians xii, "We are all one body, yet every member has its own work, whereby it serves every other"; all because we have one baptism, one Gospel, one faith, and are all alike Christians; for baptism, Gospel and faith alone make us "spiritual" and a Christian people.[4]

Luther went on to say that everyone was a priest, a bishop and a pope. He considered that a priest was nothing more than an office holder. "From all this it follows that there is really no difference between laymen and priests, princes and bishops, 'spirituals' and 'temporals,' as they call them, except that of office and work, but not the 'estate'; for they are all of the same estate—true priests, bishops and popes—though they are not all engaged in the same work, just as all priests and monks have not the same work." Luther then attacked rather strongly those persons who had placed the power in the hands of the spirituals to dictate policy and reform the temporals. Luther on the other hand places the power to reform the Church in the hands of the secular authorities. "On this account the Christian temporal power should exercise its office without let or hindrance, regardless whether it be pope, bishop, or priest whom it affects; whoever is guilty, let him suffer. All that the Canon Law has said to the contrary is sheer invention of Roman presumption." Luther believed that temporal power was ordained of God, and that the temporal authorities had the right and duty to punish evildoers regardless of their office or work.[5]

With the attack on the First Wall Luther thought he had demolished one of the main theories of the Romanists—namely, the supremacy of the ecclesiastical authorities over the secular. He denounced the idea that there was any real difference between spiritual and temporal rulers. All baptized Christians are spiritual. The only difference between baptized Christians is found in the office that the individuals performs. Members of the clergy should not be treated any differently from any other individual or person. If a member of the clergy did wrong, he should be punished in the same manner as a peasant or shoemaker who had committed the same evil. No wonder many of the princes of Germany looked with such favor on this political tract of Luther. If some of the injunctions were followed, it would place in their hands considerable power over the church.

With the destruction of the First Wall, Luther then proceeded to demolish the remaining two: interpretation of Scripture belonged only to the Pope, and only the Pope could call a council. With these torn down he could turn to what councils should discuss as far as abuses were concerned. However, since the topics which the councils would discuss concerned mainly the Church and not the temporal authorities, it is sufficient to repeat that Luther considered it within the province of the secular rulers to take measures to correct the abuses if the Church was unable to accomplish this. Among the abuses were: worldliness of the Pope; advisability of having such officers as cardinals; decreasing the number within the curia; abolition of annates, and here Luther enjoined the secular rulers to take a direct hand in abolishing these; plus a number of others purely of an ecclesiastical nature which need not concern us.

Next comes the reformatory portion of the *Address to the German Nobility*. Luther listed 27 proposals for reform necessary for the church and for the German nation. Of these 27 almost half concerned politics or were reforms where the temporal authorities should act in order to carry out the reform. Luther said, "Now, although I am too small a man to make propositions which might affect a reform in this dreadful state of things, nevertheless I may as well sing my fool's song to the end, and say, so far as I am able, what could and should be done by the temporal authorities or by a general council."[6]

In the first proposal Luther enjoins the princes, noblemen, and cities to forbid the paying of annates to Rome. Actually annates should be abolished entirely. Luther considered that the annates were robbery, and were injurious to the whole German nation. It was the duty of the temporal authorities to protect the innocent people and to prevent injustice. In the second proposal Luther went even further and urged the nobility to prohibit the papacy from making appointments in Germany. He claimed that the papacy sold these appointments to the detriment of the German nation and the church in Germany.

> Therefore, the Christian nobility should set itself against the Pope as against a common enemy and destroyer of Christendom, and should do this for the salvation of the poor souls who must go to ruin through his tyranny. They should ordain, order, and decree that henceforth no beneficies shall be drawn into the hands of Rome, and that hereafter no appointment shall be obtained there in any manner whatsoever, but that the beneficies shall be brought out and kept out from under this tyrannical authority; and they should restore to the ordinaries the right and office of ordering these beneficies in the German nation as best they may.[7]

In proposal three Luther also denied the right of confirmation of the Pope to various ecclesiastical offices. He stated that an imperial law should be made to restore the procedure of confirmation of dignity as found in the ordinances of the Council of Nicaea whereby for example a bishop was confirmed by the two nearest bishops. Luther admitted that there might be cases which could come before the Pope. But he denied that every little case should be brought to Rome. The Pope had more serious and pressing duties that needed his attention, and where possible, the Pope should not be bothered.

Luther really got to the heart of the matter concerning the temporal authorities versus the papacy when in proposal four he stated, "It should be decreed that no temporal matter shall be taken to Rome, but that all such cases shall be left to the temporal authorities, as the Romans themselves decree in that Canon Law of theirs, which they do not keep."[8] And here he defined albeit generally, what was the proper province of the temporal authorities. Money, property, life and honor were the chief concern of the secular rulers. Anything touching these things was not the concern of the spiritual rulers. Spiritual goods, according to Luther, were not money, nor anything pertaining to the body, but they were faith and good works. Luther objected to cases being taken to Rome also for quite a different reason. Here one can see a nascent German nationalism. He believed that cases tried in Rome were not fairly tried. Not only did it increase the cost by taking it all the way to Rome, but also the judges in Rome were not familiar with the local customs and laws. Decisions were based on Roman law and Roman opinion, and this could and did frequently cause injustice. So cases should be tried in the respective countries where local laws, customs, and conditions were known to the judges, and where these could be considered in handing down a decision.

In proposal nine Luther continued on the subject of Pope and Emperor.

> The Pope should have no authority over the emperor, except that he anoints and crowns him at the altar, just as a bishop anoints and crowns a king. . . . The chapter, "Solite,"

in which the papal authority is raised above the imperial authority, is not worth a heller, nor are any of those who rest upon it or fear it; for it does nothing else than force the holy words of God out of their true meaning, and wrest them to human dreams, as I have showed in a Latin treatise.

It is also ridiculous and childish that the pope, with such perverted and deluded reasoning, boasts in his decretal "Pastoralis," that he is rightful heir to the Empire, in case of a vacancy. Who has given him this right? . . . Of the same sort is also the unheard-of lie about the "Donation of Constantine." It must have been some special plague of God that so many people of understanding have let themselves be talked into accepting such lies as these, which are so manifest and clumsy that I should think any drunken peasant could lie more adroitly and skillfully. How can a man rule an empire and at the same time continue to preach, study, pray and care for the poor? Yet these are the duties which properly and peculiarly belong to the Pope.[9]

Luther was not through with the attempts of the Romanists to gain secular power. In Italy the papacy was one of the great landlords, and the Pope in fact was a territorial prince having control and sovereignty over large portions of central Italy. As Pope he had a dual role, head of the Church and temporal ruler over the States of the Church in Italy. Luther also attacked this position. Again he used the same arguments. How could a man be head of the Church and at the same time the ruler of states? Luther advised the Pope to give up these temporal holdings:

The Pope should restrain himself, take his fingers out of the pie, and claim no title to the Kingdom of Naples and Sicily. He has exactly as much right to that kingdom as I have, and yet he wishes to be its overlord. It is plunder got by violence, like almost all his other possessions. The emperor, therefore, should not grant him his fief, and if it has been granted, he should no longer give his consent to it, and should point him instead to the Bible and the prayer-books, so that he may preach and pray, and leave to temporal lords the ruling of lands and peoples, especially when no one has given them to him.

The same opinion should hold as regards Bologna, Imola, Vincenza, Ravenna, and all the territories in the Mark of Ancona, in Romagna, and in other Italian lands, which the Pope has taken by force and possesses without right. Moreover, he has meddled in these things against all the commands of Christ and St. Paul. For thus saith St. Paul, "No one entangleth himself with worldly affairs, whose business it is to wait upon the divine knighthood." No pope should be the head and front of this knighthood, yet he meddles in worldly affairs more than any emperor or king."[10]

In these two proposals, nine and ten, Luther was advocating the complete breakdown of the temporal power of the Pope, particularly in Italy. For centuries the papacy had been building up its power and authority in the Apennine Peninsula. And this was to contiune long after Luther was gone. He gave no recognition to that land deeded to the papacy through wills and such. Everything held by the Pope as a temporal ruler should be abandoned. This was a mighty blast against the worldly pretensions of the papacy. And Luther spelled out his objections in clear terms. However, the papal states in Italy were to continue for a long time after Luther.

After these blasts against the papacy as a temporal power, Luther then turned to a number of reforms within the Church itself. Such things as marriage of the clergy, decrease in the number of mendicant orders, pilgrimages to Rome, were discussed and attacked. For example, in proposal 17 he denounced the use of the interdict and the ban. The interdict was one of the most potent weapons of the papacy and the Church against recalcitrant nobles and states. But Luther claimed that the interdict should be abolished. This was an invention of the evil spirit. The ban although not abolished should be used only in very restricted and clearly defined cases. No state or entire land should be forbidden the sacraments or church offices merely because of the errors of the ruler. Although the interdict was used sparingly throughout the history of the Church, yet it was a potent weapon particularly as a threat to the obstinate who refused to obey the dictates of Rome in secular affairs.

In proposal 25 Luther took to task the law.

> The temporal law—God help us! What a wilderness it has become. Though it is much better, wiser, and more rational than the spiritual law which has nothing good about it except the name, still there is far too much of it. Surely the Holy Scriptures and good rulers would be law enough; as St. Paul says in I Corinthians vi, "Is there no one among you who can judge his neighbor's cause, that ye must go to law before heathen courts?" It seems just to me that territorial laws and territorial customs should take precedence of the general imperial laws, and the imperial laws be used only in case of necessity. Would to God that as every land has its own peculiar character, so it were ruled by its own brief laws, as the lands were ruled before these imperial laws were invented, and many lands are still ruled without them! These diffuse and far-fetched laws are only a burden to the people, and hinder causes more than they help them. I hope, however, that others have given this matter more thought and attention than I am able to do.[11]

Luther here, as he did in 1525 during the Peasants' War, refused to discuss in detail the reform of the law or the actual right or content of the law. When the Twelve Articles of the Peasants in Swabia were presented to Luther for comment, he refused to discuss certain of the articles because he was not a lawyer but merely a theologian. Here in the proposal for reform of the secular law, Luther said again that reform was necessary, and that the law of the land in particular areas should be used more and the imperial law only when necessary. How this should come about was not stated. He was merely pointing up the necessity for reform; others more competent and knowledgeable must do this work.

It is necessary to quote rather extensively from proposal 26 because Luther discussed the Pope and the Holy Roman Empire. In this proposal he condemned the ardent Roman party for its pretensions to temporal power, and strongly disapproved of the past actions of the Romanists in oppressing German emperors, and criticized it for the shabby treatment that these emperors received at the hands of the papacy. And he considered that these actions were all contrary to the Holy Gospel. Luther explained how the Pope was able to gain control of the empire. When the Pope could not subdue the emperor at Constantinople, the Pope thought of the device of giving the title of emperor to the warlike Germans as a fief. As a result the good Germans became servants of the Pope. However, the Pope had since driven out the German emperor from Rome, and he had forbidden the emperor to reside in the eternal city. As a result the Germans had the name, but the Romanists had the land and the cities. "They have always abused our simplicity to serve their own arrogance and tyranny, and they call us mad Germans, who let ourselves be made apes and fools at their bidding."[12] Even though the empire was given to the Germans by evil men, it still was through the Providence of God. Luther did not advise the Germans to give up the empire. They should retain it, and rule it wisely and in the fear of God. And he went even farther. "If it is true (that the Pope has given us the empire), then let the Pope give us Rome and everything else which he has got from the empire; let him free our land from his intolerable taxing and robbing, and give us back our liberty, authority, wealth, honor, body and soul; let the empire be what an empire should be, and let his words and pretensions be fulfilled."[13] Luther wanted the emperor to be truly emperor without let or hindrance. Let the papacy not be excepted from the dominion of the emperor and refuse to allow the Romanists to direct the temporal sword. That is the role of the emperor.

In the last proposal Luther concentrated on the failings of the temporal estate. Here he spoke as a social and economic reformer. He suggested five basic areas of reform which were the province and concern of the temporal authorities. The first was the need for a general law and decree of the German nation against extravagance and luxury in dress. This was a cause of much impoverishment among the nobles and former rich men. The emphasis on silks, ornaments, and other luxuries in dress had caused envy and desires on the part of the people to be like and equal to others. It had caused the rise of domestic robbers within Germany in the guise of merchants; particularly the velvet and silk merchants. The second area of reform was the restriction of the spice traffic. Germany produced enough good things to eat which were choice and good. Luther claimed not to be opposed to commerce, yet he said that not many good customs had come to a people through commerce. He pointed out that in ancient times God made His People of Israel dwell away from the sea on this account, and he did not let them engage in commerce. In the third area of reform he returned to the attack on annuities, which he later, in 1524, in his tract on trade and usury, was to denounce so vehemently. He advised that the Fuggers and similar corporations be checked. "I do not understand how a man with a hundred gulden can make a profit of twenty gulden in one year, nay, how with one gulden he can make another."[14] Some aspects of the rising capitalism of 16th century Europe were too much for Martin Luther. He was a strong advocate of agriculture and cattle-raising. These were the occupations favored by God. He said that there was still much land untilled, and a great deal for man to do on the land. He should not spend so much time on commerce, but should return to the land. In area four he condemned the Germans for their reputation as excessive eaters and drinkers. Germans had a bad reputation in foreign lands. Preaching could not stop it; it had become too common and had got the upper hand among the people. The temporal sword could do something, and it should. The reformer implied that some laws or decrees were necessary and that they should be rigidly enforced. And he finally took up the social evils present. Open and common houses of prostitution should be eliminated. If the people of Israel could exist without such abominations, why could not Christians do as much?

With the discussion of the failings of the temporal estate and what they should do and needed to do, Luther closed this extensive tract on reform and on politics. He did mention a previous work to which the readers might refer in which he outlined Good Works for Rulers (this is also the title):[15]

> Three special, distinct works all rulers might do in our times, particularly in our lands. First, to make an end of the horrible gluttony and drunkenness, not only because of the excess, but also because of its expense. For through seasoning and spices and the like, without which men could well live, no little loss of temporal wealth has come and daily is coming upon our lands. To prevent these two great evils would truly give temporal power enough to do, for the inroads they have made are wide and deep. And how could those in power serve God better and thereby also improve their own land?
>
> Secondly, to forbid the excessive cost of clothing whereby so much wealth is wasted and yet only the world and the flesh are served; it is fearful to think that such abuse is to be found among the people who have been pledged, baptized, and consecrated to Christ, the Crucified, and who should bear the Cross after Him and prepare for the life to come by dying daily. If some erred through ignorance, it might be borne; but that it is practised so freely, without punishment, without shame, without hindrance, and that praise and fame, are sought thereby, that is indeed an unchristian thing. Thirdly, to drive out the usurious buying of rent-charges, which in the whole world ruins, consumes and troubles all lands, peoples, and cities through its cunning form, by which it appears not to be usury, while in truth it is worse than usury, because men are not on their guard against it as against open usury. See, these are the three Jews, as men say, who suck the whole world dry. Here princes ought not to sleep, nor be lazy, if they would give a good account of their office to God.[16]

The *Address to the Nobility of the German Nation* is considered the primary work of Martin Luther on political matters. This was one of the three great literary works produced in the year 1520.[17] One can ask the question after the above examination of

this great thunderous work, Just what are the powers of the
temporal authorities and what are the powers of the Church?
The answer has to be that in matters concerning life, property,
and wealth, the State is supreme. Matters concerning the soul and
the soul alone are under the control of the Church. Each in a
sense is separate. At least, Luther considered them so. But was
there to be a separation of Church and State as we understand
it in the 20th century? What of Luther's proposals for reform in
the *Address to the German Nobility* where he allotted the right
of reform to the secular rulers in case the ecclesiastical authorities
did not themselves carry out the reform? When the Church organization was lax in the matter of reform, then the secular rulers
could and must step into the picture. In his letter to Nicholas
Amsdorf, which accompanied the *Address*, Luther stated clearly
his reasons for writing this tract and also hinted at the powers
of the laity in church affairs. "The time to keep silence has passed
and the time to speak is come, as saith Ecclesiastes. I have followed our intention and brought together some matters touching
the reform of the Christian Estate, to be laid before the Christian
Nobility of the German Nation, in the hope that God may deign
to help His Church through the efforts of the laity, since the
clergy, to whom this task more properly belongs, have grown
quite indifferent."[18] He went on to say that in the past, councils
had made various attempts at reformation, but these councils
had been unsuccessful. It was now necessary for the secular lords
to take a hand in this pressing and urgent matter. Luther actually
was giving the laity wide powers in relation to the Church. However, this was not unique in German history. When the German
emperors in the past, such as Frederick I and Frederick II, strong
men, had attempted to control the Church, the ardent papal
party had even come to be strong advocates of what might be
called separation of Church and State, and a distinct definition of
their respective powers. When the German emperors had been
weak, the Romanists had come out strongly for strong ties between Church and State. In the one case there had been a fear
of state domination; in the other there had been the hope of
church domination of the state. Thus political conditions of the
day had determined to a great extent how far either the secular

or spiritual authorities would go in their claims and temporal pretensions.

Obviously Martin Luther considered the State to be a divine institution, ordained by God to rule the Kingdom of the World. In his tract written in 1523, *Secular Authority to What Extent It Should Be Obeyed*,[19] he expanded on this point that the State was a divine institution. He divided the population of the world, the Children of Adam, into two classes. The first belonged to the Kingdom of God; the second to the Kingdom of the World. Those who belonged to the first class were all true believers and were subjects of Christ. They needed no laws, since they had within themselves the Holy Spirit which instructed them, and they could do no wrong. If all the people were members of this first class, there would be no need for secular law or for the secular sword. Unfortunately, however, not all people were true believers. In fact, the majority of people belonged to the Kingdom of the World. Even though they might call themselves Christian, in reality they were not Christians at all.

> Since few believe, and still fewer live a Christian life, do not resist evil, and themselves do no evil, God has provided for non-Christians a different government outside the Christian estate and God's kingdom, and has subjected them to the sword, so that even though they would do so, they cannot practice their wickedness, and that if they do, they may not do it without fear nor in peace and prosperity . . . For this reason God has ordained the two governments: the spiritual, which by the Holy Spirit under Christ makes Christians and pious people; and the secular, which restrains the unchristian and the wicked so that they must needs keep peace outwardly, even against their will.[20]

Luther then went on to give a gloomy picture of what would happen if the secular sword were removed because people claimed they were Christians and needed no restraint. Chaos would result. The poor and weak would be destroyed by the strong. Here Luther had in mind the false teachings of men like Münzer, who did not understand the value of secular government.

Münzer also erred in his interpretation of the political teachings of the Gospel and the extremely important pronouncements by the Apostles Paul and Peter. For this reason too, the two kingdoms must be sharply distinguished and both permitted to remain. The one, the Kingdom of God, produced piety; the other brought external peace and prevented evil deeds. Neither was sufficient in the world without the other. No one could become pious before God by means of the secular government, without Christ's spiritual rule. But Luther clearly pointed out that all were subject to the secular authority. Especially was this true with the real Christians: "Because the sword is a very great benefit and necessary to the whole world to preserve peace, to punish sin and to prevent evil, he (the true believer) submits most willingly to the rule of the sword, pays taxes, honors those in authority, serves, helps, and does all he can to further the government, that it may be sustained and held in honor and fear."[21]

The State according to Luther was then a coercive instrument. It was an institution ordained by God to bring about external peace on earth. It had the power of the law and the power of the sword to carry out its purpose. The State was to prevent evil and punish sin. But the State too was to protect its subjects; however, we shall examine later what a good ruler should do and what he should be. The duties of the subjects could be simply stated: obedience. But there were limitations to this obedience which shall be examined later. The primary duty of the subject was to obey the divinely instituted authority, and to submit to injustice when present, and to be a martyr rather than resist God's ordained rulers on earth. Luther took a pessimistic attitude toward government and toward people in general. Since the beginning there had been murder, chaos, and various unchristian acts, and he semed to be saying that people had changed little in that time. The majority were still non-Christians in their actions and beliefs even though they might profess themselves to be Christian. As a result, a coercive state was necessary. Man was born in sin, and remained in sin.

As in other instances, Luther devoted many pasages in sermons, letters, and tracts to political matters. In 1524 he wrote an interesting tract on education, *To the Councilmen of all Cities in Germany that They Should Establish and Maintain Christian Schools.*[22] As the title indicates, Luther is critical of the need for education of the young. He considered it the duty and responsibility of the civil authorities to provide proper education for the young people of Germany. In 1530 he enlarged on this theme when he completed and published *A Sermon on Keeping Children in School.*[23] Again, as in the earlier tracts, Luther considers it the duty and responsibility of the civil authorities to provide proper education facilities for the young. What had once been the exclusive preserve of the church, was now the task of the magistrates of the cities.

Luther's writings on education, already mentioned above, demonstrate that the Reformer was taking part in that trend in 16th century Europe; the increasing power of the state vis-à-vis the church. In the Middle Ages much that we would consider the province of the state was under the control of the church. Education was such a case. The great educational institutions of Europe were all church controlled and operated. Luther was, as was seen above, to advocate breaking this monopoly and placing more and more authority in the hands of the civil government. Caution is necessary, however, in attributing this to Luther's modernity.

8.

LUTHER'S POLITICS: PART TWO

As was seen above, Martin Luther wrote prodigiously on political matters. Most of his great political treatises were produced in the momentous year 1520, but even after that year he continued to expound and to enlighten his followers and readers on purely political problems. He admitted that there were really few Christians in the world during his lifetime. The members of the Kingdom of God needed no coercive authority over them to supervise their lives. They already lived according to the Gospel and were imbued with the Holy Spirit. But these Christians were definitely in the minority. The vast majority of the people of the world comprised that worldly kingdom. Since these had inherited the sins of their forefathers, authority was needed to prevent them from surrendering to their base nature. As a result, God had ordained that worldly governments should exist to provide order in the world.

The State was thus a divine institution with a very important role to play. Not only was it to provide order on earth, but it was to protect the innocent and weak from the strong and power-seeking people. The worldly governments were armed with the secular sword which was to be wielded to provide this peace, prosperity, and security for all the subjects and citizens of this worldly kingdom. The State was also to punish the guilty, and although Luther advocated mercy in dealing with the guilty, nevertheless the punishment was to be severe in order to forestall other evil persons from committing further depredations or illegal acts against the State.

The key to all of the political writings of Luther can be found in the single word: obedience. He had a tremendously high opinion of the State, although he certainly was not blind to the excesses and faults of various princes and rulers in positions of authority. During the Peasants' War, he had taken to task the princes themselves for causing many of the conditions which led the poor peasants to revolt. Luther was no shrinking violet when it came to criticism of secular authority. But one can clearly see Luther's high opinion of the temporal rulers and the role of obedience in a tract which he wrote in 1520, *A Brief Explanation of the Ten Commandments, the Creed, and the Lord's Prayer.*[1] Naturally, the bulk of this treatise is devoted to purely religious matters. But in the discussion of the Ten Commandments he touched on the subject of the obligations to the State. In the discussion of the fourth commandment he said, "The Second Table of Moses—the Table of the Left Hand—contains the other seven

Commandments. In these man is taught what he is in duty bound to do and not to do to other men, that is to his neighbor. The first of these (the fourth Commandment) teaches how one is to conduct oneself toward all the authorities who are God's representatives. Therefore, it has its place before the rest and immediately after the first three, which concern God himself. Such authorities are father and mother, spiritual and temporal lords, etc." In the first three commandments man is taught how to act toward God, what one is to do and not to do. After these and next in importance is the commandment concerning obedience to all authority which are God's representatives on earth. Nothing could be clearer than this exposition of a subject's duty to his lords whether they be spiritual or temporal. Luther even discussed those who transgressed this commandment and listed those people who sinned against this injunction. He said, "He who does not pay honor, allegiance and obedience to his lords and those in authority, be they good or bad." No matter what kind of person the secular ruler might be, the subject's first concern should be obedience. This tract was published in 1520 and received wide circulation. Nothing could be clearer than Luther's attitude as expressed in this treatise. This tract combined with previous writings clearly showed that Luther believed that a subject owed his lord obedience and this was enjoined in the fourth commandment.

Yet for all of Luther's exposition on the State, on the duties of the subjects and duties of the lords, and particularly for his vehement stand against disobedience of any kind, the Reformer became one of the central figures in three swift and terrible revolts in the 1520's; revolts which had serious consequences for the reform movement which he headed and for the person of Luther himself. From 1521 to 1525 he unwillingly was intimately associated with the Wittenberg Disturbances, the Knights' Revolt, and the Great Peasants' War. It is ironic that a man who wrote tract after tract about secular authority, warning subjects against insurrection, condemning them for even considering such a step, should have been in the center of these same revolts. For a time Luther tried to appease both sides, attempting to take a middle ground. But when secular authority was threatened, Luther's only recourse was to side with the government against the rebels. He was condemned by the peasants for taking the opposite side, and yet with any knowledge at all of Luther's beliefs and political ideas, it could have been seen that Luther's future actions were inevitable. He was criticized for fomenting the rebellion; that he somehow had goaded the peasants in taking such action. Yet there was nothing in all of his writings, letters, or sermons, which could remotely be considered a license for revolt. On the contrary, the opposite was true.

If Luther believed that all citizens should obey the government in all things, with a limitation to be examined later, how could changes be brought about within a state when conditions reached the intolerable stage? Certainly there had to be some mechanism or outline which the subjects could follow when they were ruled by a tyrant who oppressed them, took their land and wealth, stripped them of all worldly possessions, and left them nothing. Luther did have an answer to all this. In 1522, after his return to Wittenberg, he delivered eight sermons in a successful attempt to stop the strife and to dispel the seeds of revolt which had gathered during his absence. In those eight sermons he gave a partial answer to the question of change. He had chastized the citizenry of Wittenberg by taking matters into their own hands. He told them that they should have gone to the proper authorities (in this case the Town Council) and requested that the changes be enacted. This was the orderly and lawful manner to bring about changes which even he, Luther, seemed to favor. It was improper and illegal to force the changes through by violence and coercion. A delegation should have met with members of the town council, made proposals, and then waited for action. However, Luther stressed that even if no action had been taken on the proposals, the citizenry should have refrained from violence. Once the legal and proper methods had been tried, everything was in the hands of God after that. If nothing was done to alleviate conditions, the people should suffer in silence knowing that they were doing a pleasing thing in the eyes of the Lord.

However, some of Luther's statements on the problem of rebellion itself must be examined. As a result of disturbing reports which reached him late, the Reformer had written a very important tract on rebellion, *An Earnest Exhortation for All Christians, Warning them against Insurrection and Rebellion.*[2] It seems that the treatise was written sometime in December, 1521, but the publication was delayed until January, 1522, before his return from the Wartburg. This tract was devoted mainly to the question of revolt against the Papacy and the Romanists; however, Luther did generalize concerning revolts of any kind. And he was very explicit in his statements. Concerning reform of the Church he said:

Even if the occurrence of an insurrection were possible, and God were willing to visit so gracious a punishment upon them, insurrection is an unprofitable method of procedure, and never results in the desired reformation. For insurrection is devoid of reason and generally hurts the innocent more than the guilty. Hence no insurrection is ever right, no matter how good the cause in whose interest it is made. The harm resulting from it always exceeds the amount of reformation accomplished, so that it fulfills the saying, "Things go from bad to worse." For this reason temporal powers are ordained and the sword is given into their hands that they may punish the wicked and protect the godly, and that insurrection may not be necessary, as St. Paul says in Romans xiii, and also St. Peter in I Peter ii. But when Sir Mob breaks loose he cannot tell the wicked from the godly nor keep them apart; he strikes at random, and then horrible injustice is inevitable.[3]

Again Luther clearly stated his own position if and when insurrection should occur. He said, "My sympathies are and always will be with those against whom insurrection is made, however wrong the cause they stand for, and opposed to those who make the insurrection, however much they may be in the right. For there can be no insurrection without the shedding of innocent blood and wrong done to the guiltless."[4] What possibly could be clearer than this statement? Luther never deviated from this position, and any individual reading the treatise at the time or later in the 1520's could easily have foretold what Luther's position would be in the case of a rebellion against the legally constituted authorities.[5]

In the year 1525, Luther wrote *An Open Letter concerning the Hard Book Against the Peasants.*[6] In this rather brief treatment he gives his reaction to the rebel, and refers to his second pamphlet:

> My little book was not written against simple evildoers, but against rebels. You must make a very, very great distinction between rebel and a thief, or a murderer, or any other kind of evil-doer. For a murderer, or other evil-doer, lets the head of the government alone, and attacks only the members of their property; nay he fears the ruler. So long as the head remains, no one ought to attack such a murderer, because the head can punish him, but everyone ought to await the judgement and command of the head, to whom God has committed the sword and the office of punishment. But a rebel attacks the head himself and interferes with his sword and his office, and therefore his crime is not to be compared with that of a murderer. He cannot wait until the head gives command and passes judgement, for the head is himself captured and beaten and cannot give them, but everyone who can must run, uncalled and unbidden, and as a true member, help to rescue his head by thrusting, hewing, and killing, and risk his life and goods for the head's sake. See, now! A rebel is a man who runs upon his head and lord with naked sword. No one should wait, then, until his lord bids him prevent it, but the first who can ought to run in and stab the rascal unbidden, and not worry whether he is committing murder; for he has only kept off an arch-murderer, who wanted to murder the whole land. . . For rebellion is no jest, and there is no evil deed on earth that compares with it. Other wicked deeds are single acts; rebellion is a Noah's flood of wickedness.

> I am called a clergyman and have the office of the Word,

but if I were the servant even of a Turk and saw my lord in danger I would forget my spiritual office and thrust and hew as long as I had a heartbeat left. If I were slain in doing, I should go straight to heaven. For rebellion is a crime that deserves no other court nor mercy, whether it be among heathen, Jews, Turks, Christians, or any other people; it is already heard, judged, condemned, and sentenced to death at anybody's hands. There is nothing to do about it, except to kill quickly, and give the rebel his deserts. No murderer does so much evil, and none deserves so much evil. For a murderer commmits a penal offense, and lets the penalty stand; but a rebel tries to make wickedness free and unpunishable, and attacks the punishment itself.[7]

One could go on and on quoting from the various political writings of Luther in reference to rebellion. But enough has been quoted already to show his beliefs and ideas. If one examines the writings of Luther during 1525, before, and after as well, the same theme is repeated over and over. Rebellion was worse than murder or any other evil deed. It was a device of the devil; it was against God's Commandments.

Since force and violence of any kind were to be removed as a means to bring about change within the State, what methods then could the people use and what was at their disposal to bring this about? In the same treatise, *An Earnest Exhortation Against Insurrection,* Luther listed three things which the people could do in case the legally constituted authority refused to act to bring about better conditions or to bring about a reformation. According to him these three things were:

1. To confess one's own sins.
2. To pray.
3. To proclaim the Gospel.

Luther was saying the people must recognize their own sins first and must attempt to correct and eliminate these sins. Otherwise greater trouble would be visited upon them. With prayer the people would be able to invoke the help of God against wrongdoers, and by preaching the Gospel ardently the evil-doers could be slain with words. Luther claims that an armed insurrection was unnecessary. For he says that Christ had already started an insurrection with his mouth which the papal authorities would not be able to bear.[8] It is true that the above tract was written in reference to the reports of religious disturbances which Luther had received, and he was quite concerned about the excesses and abuses which might arise among the radicals. However, he was such a staunch advocate of legally constituted authority that the arguments which he presents in this tract can equally be applied to insurrection against the State. A close examination of any and all of his other political writings will bear this out.

Nevertheless Luther continued to be bothered about the question of secular authorities going too far in the use of their own power. And the question naturally arose as to when secular authority could be disobeyed. In 1523, after much thought and contemplation, Luther wrote, *On Secular Authority To What Extent it Should be Obeyed.*[9] Here he examined the extent of temporal power and decided that there were limits to this power and were limits to the subjects' obligations to his lord. When the rulers exceeded their power, the subjects were no longer bound to obey them. This was a remarkable statement by Luther. However, it must be reiterated that the subjects in no conditions were to revolt, rebel or use force in their disobedience. They were to submit to the tyranny and the unjust actions of the secular lords even if the rulers were to use violence. In this treatise we find an example where disobedience was urged on the people.

Again Luther repeats that the children of Adam were divided into two kingdoms. The children of the Kingdom of God needed no secular authority over them since they were the true Christians and live their lives according to the Gospel in harmony with each other, and no coercion was necessary. Among true Christians there was no evil and no evil-doers. No laws were necessary, and the secular sword was inapplicable here. But governments were ordained by God for the great mass of people. These were the unbelievers, not the true Christians, who needed authority over them to make them live in peace and harmony with each other.

Luther painted an interesting picture of what would happen if all the world were to be ruled by the Gospel, with true believers outnumbered by the unbelievers. It would be like having wolves and lions among a sheepfold.

> If any one attempted to rule the world by the Gospel, and put aside all secular law and the secular sword, on the plea that all are baptised and Christian, and that according to the Gospel, there is among them neither law nor sword, nor necessity for either, pray what would happen? He would loose the bands and chains of the wild and savage beasts, and let them tear and mangle everyone, and at the same time say they were quite tame and gentle creatures; but I would have proof in my wounds. Just so would the wicked under the name of Christian abuse this freedom of the Gospel, carry on their knavery, and say that they were Christians subject neither to law nor sword, as some are already raving and ranting.[10]

Luther then takes up his central theme:

> We now come to the main part of this treatise. For as we have learned that there must be temporal authority on earth, and how it is to be employed in a Christian and salutary way, we must now learn how far its arm extends and how far its hand reaches, lest it extend too far and encroach upon God's kingdom and rule. And it is very necessary to know this, since where it is given too wide a scope, intolerable and terrible injury follows; and, on the other hand, it cannot be too much restricted without working injury. In the latter case the punishment is too light; in the former, too severe. It is more tolerable, however, to err on the latter side and punish too little; since it is always better to let a knave free than to kill a good man, for the world will still have knaves, and must have them, but of good men there are few.[11]

Luther said that every kingdom must have its own laws and regulations, and without law no kingdom or government could exist. Worldly government had laws which extended no farther than to life and property and what was external upon earth. Over the soul God could and would let no one rule but himself. Therefore, when temporal power presumed to prescribe laws for the soul, it encroached upon God's domain, and this only misled and destroyed the souls. And Luther hoped that this was so clear that everyone could understand it, and that the rulers, including princes and bishops, might know what fools they were when they tried to coerce the people with their laws and commandments into believing one thing or another. Here he seemed to be espousing religious freedom. Let every man worship as he wished.

> When a man-made law is imposed upon the soul, in order to make it believe this or that, as that man prescribes, there is certainly no word of God for it . . . Hence it is the height of folly when they command that one shall believe the Church (or Church Organization), the fathers, the councils, though there be no word of God for it . . . No one shall and can command the soul, unless he can show it the way to heaven; but this no man can do, only God. Therefore, in matters which concern the salvation of souls nothing but God's Word shall be taught and accepted.[12]

Here again Luther was dividing the temporal and spiritual powers and giving them separate and distinct authority. Where the temporal power attempted to control the soul or to order the soul, then it had extended its power too far. It could tax the people, punish the guilty, and carry out laws which extended to property and life, and that was all. What happened when a tyrant did attempt to extend his authority beyond the scope which Luther had outlined? Here Luther had the answer. Here a subject might and rightfully so, disobey his lord and master. He must not use force or violence. He was not to defend himself or his property against the lord.

If then your prince or temporal lord commands you to

hold with the pope, to believe this or that, or commands you to give up certain books, you should say, "It does not befit Lucifer to sit by the side of God. Dear lord, I owe you obedience with life and goods; command me within the limits of your power on earth, and I will obey. But if you command me to believe, and to put away books, I will not obey; for in this case you are a tyrant and over-reach yourself, and command where you have neither right nor power," etc. Should he take your property for this, and punish such obedience, blessed are you. Thank God that you are worthy to suffer for the sake of the divine Word, and let him rave, fool that he is. He will meet his judge. For I tell you, if you do not resist him but give him his way, and let him take your faith or your books, you have really denied God.[13]

Luther then gave an illustration of what was happening in certain places throughout Germany. Some tyrants were ordering their subjects to deliver to the courts copies of the New Testament. And he urged the people in this case not to deliver even a single page of the New Testament. On the contrary, the people were to refuse to give up anything to the courts. However, if their houses were searched and books and goods taken by force, the people were to allow this injustice. No violence or resistance by force was to be employed. Outrage was to be endured. These tyrants and unjust rulers would be punished by God. Thus when Luther spoke of resistance, he did not mean by force. The people were to tell the rulers they were being unjust or acting contrary to the laws of God. If the tyrant persisted, the subjects were to allow the lords to take everything if they wanted that. Acquiescence at least in actions was the key here. Obey the lord in all things which he had a right to command. Refuse obedience when the temporal authorities overstepped their power, but do not take active measures to show disobedience.

In the above discussion of the State, as found in the writings of Martin Luther, it is discernible that to the Reformer the State was a divine institution, ordained by God to rule over things of the world, the world of the flesh or as Luther repeated so many

times, the Kingdom of the World. The State was a necessary institution, which demanded the respect, obedience, and allegiance
of the people within or subject to the State. Since it was a divine
institution, Luther proved by constant reference to the Gospel
that the peoples' first duty was to obey the secular authorities.
And he further believed that changes, which were bound to come
and which at times were necessary and expedient, must and
could be brought about only by peaceful means. Only those
changes which came about through reliance on God and His
Gospel were permanent and good. However, Luther did not
advocate blind obedience, without regard to the limitations of the
State. For the Reformer definitely established limits of secular
authority, and stated categorically that when the State exceeded
these limits, then the subjects must resist. Not that they might
resist; they must resist if they were to carry out God's Commandments. But resistance was to take peaceful means. A subject could
openly refuse to obey, but he was not to resist by force the seizure
of his property or his life. It was better to lose one's life than to
resist by force the legally constituted powers, even though they
might be unjust and even though they might be exceeding their
limits as rulers of the Kingdom of the World. Luther established
for his readers a method or series of measures which they could
take in case of a tyrant. And it is significant that these tyrants
might not be all heathen. Many of them would claim to be
Christian, in that they were baptized. In fact, they were
unbelievers.

Luther was not an advocate in all cases of nonviolence, however. We have seen, for instance, that in cases of rebellion he
would take up arms himself as a clergyman to protect the rulers
who were the divinely ordained authorities. In matters, however,
of changes within a state, these changes must be orderly, without violence, and by purely peaceful and lawful methods. Yet we
must note that Luther was moderate in his views and urged
that the rulers be prudent and wise in treating subjects who
acted against the best interests of their lord. In the *Magnificat*
written in 1520, Luther treats the subjects of what a ruler should
do in case his subjects are being oppressed or threatened with

injury by others.[14] Here he urges good sense and caution on the part of the rulers.

> If a ruler did not defend his land and subjects against injustice, but followed my advice, made no resistance and let all be taken from him, what would the world come to? I will briefly set down my view of the matter. Temporal power is in duty bound to defend its subjects, as I have frequently said; for it bears the sword in order to keep in fear those who do not heed such divine teaching, and to compel them to leave others in peace. And in this the temporal power seeks not its own but its neighbor's profit and God's honor; it would gladly remain quiet and let its sword rust, if God had not ordained it to be a hindrance to the evil-doers. Yet this defense of its subjects should not be accompanied by still greater harm, that would be put to leap from the frying pan into the fire. It is a poor defense to expose a whole city to danger for the sake of one person, or to risk the entire country for a single village or castle, unless God should have enjoined this by a special command, as He did of old time. If a robber-knight robs a citizen of his property and you, my lord, lead your army against him to punish this injustice, and in so doing lay waste the whole land, who will have wrought the greater harm, the knight or the lord? David winked at many things when he was unable to punish without bringing harm upon others. All rulers must do the same. On the other hand, a citizen must endure a certain measure of suffering for the sake of the community, and not demand that all other men undergo for his sake the greater injury. . . . If men went to war on every provocation and passed by no insult, we should never be at peace and have naught, but destruction besides. Therefore, right or wrong is never a sufficient cause indiscriminately to punish or make war.[15]

Luther's moderation and conservative nature were well illustrated in this particular work, the *Magnificat*. He was essentially a man of peace, even a pacifist to a certain extent. Everything must come about through the working of the Word of God. Changes, which were inevitable, must be peaceful and gradual. Violence in any form was wrong. Even violence used to defend one's life or property was wrong and intolerable. A Christian must be willing to bear sufferings and wrongs since this was pleasing to the Lord.

In spite of all the writings of Martin Luther on political matters, it is necessary to inquire into the form of government which the Reformer favored and also to examine his ideas concerning political equality. However, one has to remember that Luther was a man of the 16th century. This was the age of the Holy Roman Empire of the German Nation, an anachronism in the age of the rising nation-state, but nevertheless it was a political organization which embodied a faith in empire shared by many, including the great Reformer in Germany. It is true that the office of emperor was elective, but only the great electors, seven at the time of Luther, were able to exercise the franchise for the selection of the emperor. Poland too was to become an elective monarchy, but the elective principle itself cannot be construed as meaning a real political democracy within these areas. Even the Swiss experiment cannot be remotely compared to 20th century political democracy. Although there were no kings, the Swiss, like the Free cities of Germany, were ruled by an oligarchy with the peasants and the lower classes in the towns having little or no say in government affairs.

In the Peasants' War, there were political demands among the various peasant groups, whether these were incorporated in the famous Twelve Articles or whether they were included in the lists of other peasant groups in Germany. One of the cries of the peasants was, "No Lord but the Emperor." This slogan was not a cry for political equality. It was a reaction to the residual feudalism in existence throughout portions of Germany, and it was an attempt on the part of the malcontents to point up or emphasize their dislike of the excesses and the heavy exactions of the local feudal lords. The emperor was considered to be a person to whom all could and should owe allegiance, and this allegiance and obedience was considered natural. It had been one of the main points of the pre-1525 revolts such as the *Amre Conrad* and the *Bundschuh* of the preceding century. By the time of the Peasants' War of 1525 the political aims of the radicals had progressed to a point where social and political equality was being demanded. For example, the Third Article of the Twelve Articles states:

> It has been the custom hitherto for men to hold us as their own property and this is pitiable, seeing that Christ has redeemed and bought us all with the precious shedding of His blood, the lowly as well as the great, excepting no one. Therefore, it agrees with Scripture that we be free and will to be so. Not that we should be entirely free; God does not teach us that we should desire no rulers. We are to live in the commandments, not in the free selfwill of the flesh; but we are to love God, recognize Him in our neighbor as our Lord, and do all (as we gladly would do) that God has commanded in the Lord's Supper; therefore, we ought to love according to His commandment. This commandment does not teach us that we are not to be obedient to the rulers, but we are to humble ourselves, not before the rulers only, but before everyone. Thus to our chosen and appointed rulers (appointed for us by God) we are willingly obedient in all proper and Christian matters, and we have no doubt that, as true and real Christians, they will gladly release us from serfdom, or show us in the Gospel that we are serfs.[16]

Here was a clearcut demand that serfdom be abolished; and that all men be regarded equal, without reference to their station or occupation in life. This was really the only one of the Twelve Articles which was concerned specifically with political affairs. Such radicals as Münzer, Gaismair, and Karlstadt, but especially Münzer, preached to the people social and political equality, and fortified these sayings with liberal quotations from the Scripture. Also it is not inconceivable that Luther's own tracts and sermons contributed much to the prevailing feeling for social and political equality among the people. In 1520 he had written *A Trea-*

tise on Christian Liberty.[17] Even though the treatise is not concerned with secular government, the term liberty or freedom was
sufficient cause for a widespread influence among the people. It
makes little or no difference that few of the peasants ever read
the tract. The fact that the leader of the reform movement advocated Freedom of the Christian was enough. After all were they
not baptized Christians? Being such they should be allowed the
liberty which Luther seemed to be expounding in this treatise.
Later he could repeat time and time again that he was not
espousing liberty of the flesh; that his freedom or liberty was
purely a spiritual matter. These explanations had little effect on
the people who had heard of the freedom of the Christian and
who also were being harassed by the flamboyant and ardent
tongue of Münzer.

It is necessary to examine two of Luther's writings to describe
his views of political and social equality and see how consistent
he was and how ardent and vehement he was in espousing his
philosophy. Since the Third Article of the Twelve Articles of the
Peasants in Swabia concerning the abolition of serfdom and its
indirect reference to equality was quoted, Luther's rather pun-
gent reply to this Third Article should be examined. In the spring
of 1525, after the Twelve Articles had been agreed upon by the
peasant conference, a copy of these was sent to Martin Luther for
examination and comment. He was asked in effect to judge these
demands or proposals and determine whether they were justified,
and if they erred in any respect Luther was to set the peasants
on the right road. He was very conciliatory and moderate in his
reply to the peasants. He was far harsher with respect to the
princes. In replying to the Third Article specifically, he categorically denied that there was anything in all his writings that could
remotely justify the idea of abolishing serfdom or calling for the
equality of all men.

"There shall be no serfs, for Christ has made all men free."
This is making Christian liberty an utterly carnal thing. Did
not Abraham and other patriarchs and prophets have slaves?
Read what St. Paul teaches about servants, who, at that time,

were all slaves. Therefore, this article is dead against the
Gospel. It is a piece of robbery by which every man takes
from his lord the body, which has become his lord's property.
For a slave can be a Christian and have Christian liberty, in
the same way that a prisoner or a sick man is a Christian, and
yet not free. This article would make all men equal, and
turn the spiritual kingdom of Christ into a worldly, external
kingdom, and that is impossible. For a worldly kingdom cannot stand unless there is in it an inequality of persons, that
some are free, some imprisoned, some lords, some subjects,
etc.; and St. Paul says in Galatians V, that in Christ master
and servant are one thing. On this subject my friend Urban
Regius has written enough; you may read further in his
book.[18]

In the above comment, Luther denies that equality can exist
in the Kingdom of the World. As he had written so many times
before, the people were divided into the Kingdom of God (the
true believers) and the Kingdom of the World (the external, carnal and evil world). In the latter, force was necessary to make
men live peacefully with one another. The peasants in Article
Three were misinterpretating the Gospel and were being led by
ambitious and evil men. Freedom was not something to be identified with the temporal or secular authorities. Freedom and
liberty of the Christian was completely spiritual. In this treatise
Luther set down and discussed two propositions: A Christian man
was a perfectly free lord of all, subject to none; and a Christian
man was a perfectly dutiful servant of all, subject to all. These
two propositions illustrated clearly Luther's attitude toward a
subject and a subject's duty to authority. Again he divided the
people of the world into the two kingdoms, a constantly recur-
ring theme, and went into great detail how the true spiritual inward man needed no authority over him since he lived according
to the Gospel. Yet for all this, the true Christian would obey all
authorities over him even though he himself needed no such
authority. But the spiritual man knew that secular authority had
been ordained by God and as such was a necessary thing. Thus

he automatically obeyed the secular power, and if necessary
would even suffer injustice and wrong done to him, his person,
or his property, since suffering was considered a part of every
Christian's life. Luther argued that no external thing whatever
had any influence on the inward, spiritual man. He said:

> What can it profit the soul if the body fare well, be free
> and active, eat, drink, and do as it pleases? For in these things
> even the most godless slaves of all the vices fare well. On the
> other hand, how will ill health or imprisonment or hunger or
> thirst or any other external misfortune hurt the soul? With
> these things even the most godly men are afflicted, and those
> who because of a clear conscience are most free. None of these
> things touch either the liberty or the bondage of the soul.
> The soul receives no benefit if the body is adorned with the
> sacred robes of the priesthood or dwells in sacred places, or
> is occupied with sacred duties, prayers, fasts, abstains from
> certain kinds of food or does any work whatsoever that can
> be done by the body and in the body.[19]

When Luther wrote or spoke of liberty, he was not thinking of
liberty in the political sense, but actually only of liberty of faith.
He said:

> As you see, it is a spiritual and true liberty, and makes our
> hearts free from all sins, laws, and mandates. . . . It is more
> excellent than all other liberty which is external, as heaven
> is more excellent than earth. . . . Finally, something must be
> added for the sake of those for whom nothing can be so well
> said that they will not spoil it by misunderstanding it, though
> it is a question whether they will understand even what shall
> here be said. There are very many who, when they hear of
> this liberty of faith, immediately turn it into an occasion for
> the flesh, and think that now all things are allowed them.
> They want to show that they are free men and Christians
> only by despising and finding fault with ceremonies, tradi-
> tions, and human laws.[20]

Luther advised the people to beware of those who refused to

obey human laws or who refused to participate in ceremonies
and justify their actions by claiming that they were free men and
Christians. It was necessary to resist those who advocated the
discontinuance of ceremonies and laws, but still necessary to be
prudent for the weak in faith who might need some external
signs.

This treatise of Christian Liberty was one of Luther's most
potent tracts written in that memorable year 1520. It was a piece
of writing which unfortunately was horribly misinterpreted by
many people within Germany and particularly within the area to
revolt a few years later. Yet there was nothing in this tract that
could be construed as giving license to the people to turn against
the legally constituted authority. One might quarrel with Luther's
interpretation of Liberty of Faith, and many did, but certainly
his liberty as expressed in this and subsequent tracts had nothing
whatsoever to do with political liberty as Münzer and other
radicals in the 1520's were to preach.

However, enough concerning Luther's concept of liberty and
equality. It is sufficient to reiterate that to the Reformer liberty
was a purely spiritual matter, and was in no way related to external or temporal affairs. But the question remains, What form
of government did Luther favor? As was seen, he was violently
opposed to political equality. He did not believe it possible in
the first place that all men could live together as equals. There
was far too much evil in the world for that. The population of
the Kingdom of the World far outnumbered that in the Kingdom of God. And the Kingdom of the World was composed of
many evil, overly ambitious men who did and would go to
extremes to gain power. Luther was very candid in acknowledg-
ing that many rulers, most of them in fact, were tyrants who
oppressed their subjects and did much injustice and harm to
those under their rule. Yet this must be endured by all. God himself would punish these men. So political equality or political
democracy was out of the question. This is not a criticism of
Luther, since there was no political democracy in existence at the
time. It is true that some of the radicals had advocated a return
to the primitive church where all men within the early Christian

community were equal and in fact even shared much of their goods in common. To Luther equality, now at least, was impossible. He had stated that slavery had existed since the time of the prophets of the Old Testament. He was not necessarily condoning slavery, but it had existed without interfering in man's freedom to believe, and this was the only freedom worthwhile.

In examining Luther's political writings in an attempt to discover the type of government which he favored, it is impossible to pinpoint any single writing or to quote any specific statement in which he came right out and said he favored such and such a political system. As was seen in the discussion of the *Address to the German Nobility,* he preferred first of all the continuation of the Holy Roman Empire of the German Nation. And further he wished to see the office of emperor continued to be held by a German prince. As long as the empire had been turned over to the Germans, it was well if it continued in German hands. God had seen to it that the empire was to be ruled by the Germans, and therefore, the German people should not give up the empire. Since Luther favored the empire, it has to be stated that he also favored monarchy within that empire. And this monarchy was to be in a sense an absolute monarchy. For the watchword was obedience; obedience at all times and in all things. Even if the subjects were not sure whether the princes or lords were correct or right; or even if they were in doubt as to whether the princes were violating the Word of God, obedience was still demanded. As we have seen, there was only one possible exception to all this for the private citizen; that was the case where the ruler demanded a subject to openly violate the commands of God, where no doubt existed. In this case and in this case alone, disobedience was allowed, but not to resort to violence or force, only a refusal to obey the ruler. If the lord persisted and used violence against the subjects, then the people were to submit to all the indignities and sufferings as Christ had done. He also insisted that unworthy persons holding offices were to be obeyed and respected as representatives of the government since government was ordained by God. But if the emperor broke his contract (*Wahlkapitulation*), he could be deposed by the princes.[21]

Many theologians and historians have insisted for centuries that Luther preferred a monarchial government above any other. All he did, however, in that direction was to support the type under which he lived. In his opinion it made little difference whether Germany had a republican or monarchial form of government. Said Luther Hess Waring in his excellent little book on Luther's political views: "Whatever the form of government—as Luther expresses no preference—civil authority is a sacred trust. To every man is to be given equal consideration and opportunity, under similar conditions." On the other hand, perhaps Waring waxes too enthusiastic in the following statement: Religious and civil liberty—of conscience, speech, and press—are inalienable rights belonging alike to every individual, subject only to the equal rights of others, the maintenance of public peace and order, and the sovereign power of the state over the external life, where it touches the lives of others."[22] That can be said for Luther's views in the year 1523, when he had not yet turned Saxony into a Lutheran state, and again in the last year of his life, when he did not care any more what the princes said about him. Most biographies of Luther portray him as a man whose ideas remained constant throughout his entire life.

Luther's political principles may be briefly summed up as follows:

1. The state was a divine institution, ordained by God as natural and necessary to man. The form or nature of government formed was a matter of human determination. However, it must be repeated that he indicated throughout his writings that his own preference was for the monarchial form of government.

2. The State possessed exclusive coercive authority. A person's status in the Church was not to affect his status in the state. The jurisdiction of the state was to apply to all subjects: ecclesiastic, layman, and heretic.

3. The object of the State was to protect the good, punish the wicked, and maintain public peace.

4. It was the duty of the State to educate youth (secular, moral, and religious); to care for the poor, and to provide protection for all.

5. Religious and civil liberty of conscience, freedom of speech and press were inalienable rights belonging to every individual, subject only to the equal rights of others.[23]

Now let us examine briefly some of the injunctions which Luther spelled out for the rulers; injunctions which if followed would provide assurance that the ruler would be governing in a Christian manner and also would insure that this ruler would enjoy the fruits of heaven after death. These are the ideals which all rulers should follow. Luther devoted the last section of his tract on Secular Authority to show how a prince should use the secular authority which was outlined in the first sections. Before giving the list of what a prince must be, Luther enjoined that those who wanted to enter the life beyond must have the law firmly in hand. "Therefore, a prince must have the law in hand as firmly as the sword, and decide in his own mind when and where the law must be applied strictly or with moderation, so that reason may always control all law and be the highest law and rule over all laws." Luther was saying in effect that the ruler must first depend on God. He then proceeded to list four things which a prince must do. In the first, Luther exhorted the princes that government was for the people. "My concern must be, not how I may rule and be haughty, but how they may be protected and defended by a good peace . . . Thus a prince should in his heart empty himself of his power and authority, and interest himself in the need of his subjects dealing with it as though it were his own need. Thus Christ did unto us; and these are the proper works of Christian love."[24]

In the second injunction Luther warned the princes to beware of the high and mighty among their councillors. They should not neglect the advice of the counselors, nor yet should they depend exclusively on them.

> Therefore, a prince should bestow only so much trust and power upon his rulers that he will still keep the reins of government in his own hand. He must keep his eyes open and give attention, and like Jehoshaphat, ride through the land and observe everywhere how the government and the law is ad-

ministered. In this way he will learn for himself that one must
not implicitly trust any man. For you have no right to think
that another will interest himself in you and your land so
deeply as you yourself, unless he be filled with the Spirit and
be a good Christian. The natural man does not do it. Since,
however, you do not know whether he is a Christian, or how
long he will remain one, you cannot safely depend on him.[25]

In the third injunction Luther advised the prince to deal justly
with evil-doers. He must be wise and prudent in meting out punishment; neither too little nor too much. "In brief, here one must
hold by the proverb, 'he cannot rule who cannot wink at faults.'
Let this, therefore, be his rule: Where wrong cannot be punished
without greater wrong, there let him waive his rights, however
just. He must not regard his own injury, but the wrong which
others must suffer as a consequence of the penalty he imposes."[26]
Again Luther was urging moderation among all the rulers. It
was better to punish too little than to punish severely and as a
result cause more harm to the innocent. God would take care of
those who in this world slipped by without the required and
necessary punishment.

In the fourth injunction Luther stated the most important of
these necessary things for a Christian prince to do:

A prince must also act in a Christian way toward his God,
that is, he must subject himself to Him in entire confidence
and pray for wisdom to rule well, as Solomon did . . . Therefore, we will close by saying briefly that a prince's duty is
fourfold: First, that toward God consists in true confidence
and in sincere prayer; second, that toward his subjects consists in love and Christian service; third, that toward his
counselors and rulers consists in an open mind and unfettered
judgements; fourth, that toward evil-doers consists in proper
zeal and firmness. Thus his state is right, outwardly and in-
wardly, pleasing to God and to the people. But he must
expect much envy and sorrow—the cross will soon rest on the
shoulders of such a ruler.[27]

Of course, it was only natural that Luther should enjoin all the people to obey the legally constituted rulers. Germany was still experiencing the vestiges of feudalism, and this was to remain for a long time to come. Luther as a subject of Frederick the Wise of Saxony, an elector of the Holy Roman Empire, had been well treated by this prince, who had, it is true, remained somewhat clear of the religious controversies raging around the head of this monk, but had intervened to the extent of providing protection and a safe refuge for Luther immediately following Worms. It is somewhat beyond the Peasants' War, but it is nevertheless interesting to inquire what was Luther's attitude when it became evident to all of electoral Saxony that the rulers of this state were being opposed by the emperor, Charles V, the greatest and supreme lord in the empire. Luther then had to enlarge his political view to the effect that disobedience to the emperor was not always wrong. In fact, he allowed the Protestant princes of Germany to band together in the Schmalkaldic League against the forces of Charles V. And further he acquiesced in the extension of the league to include many of the enemies of the Hapsburgs in Germany. This seems to be a slight contradiction of Luther's earlier statements concerning the prince's obedience and duty to the emperor. After all he had considered the knights' revolt against the greater princes a shameful affair. Yet when these greater princes began to take measures to oppose the Hapsburgs and the emperor, he agreed that some action was necessary and seemingly this was all right. In 1526 the League of Torgau had been formed by various Protestant princes including Luther's own John of Saxony[28] as a balance to the power of Ferdinand of Austria. In 1531, the Schmalkaldic League was agreed upon to enforce and protect the decisions of the Diet of Augsburg. Here events were moving on a higher level. In view of the injunction that subjects should resist in cases where the rulers were forcing disobedience to God's ordinances, he was able to justify his new position. The princes had elected the emperor and they had imposed certain terms on him. These he had to obey for the electors were very powerful in Luther's time.

9.

CONCLUSION

In the preceding chapters three major events in the life of Martin Luther following his appearance before the Imperial Diet at Worms have been examined: the Wittenberg Disturbances of 1522, the Knights' Revolt of 1522-1523, and the Great Peasants' War of 1524-1525. The political theories and the economic and social status of the Great Reformer have been examined in an attempt to show why Luther took such actions as he did during the last and most volatile and explosive of these three events, the Peasants' War. The Wittenberg Disturbances and the Knights' Revolt were analyzed to see if it could be discovered whether there was any inconsistency in Luther's actions and attitudes during the earlier revolts or uprisings; and also, if possible, to discover if any trend was evident during these earlier rebellions which would explain his actions during the 1525 affair. After all, Luther has been severely condemned on a number of accounts for his stand during the Peasants' War.

To Luther, and he expressed this so clearly that misunderstanding seems impossible, a rebel was the most evil of those who sinned against God's Commandments. And he indicated quite clearly that he, Luther, would always support the legally constituted government against the rebels, regardless of the type of government or regardless of who the rulers were. He said that he would support the Turks against their own subjects even if those subjects were Christian because the Turks were the legally constituted and authorized rulers in their domains. And he indicated in these three revolts that he would never deviate from this position, nor did he. There was never any inconsistency in this matter, and his detractors and critics have merely to read the Eight Sermons delivered at Wittenberg in 1522 as well as the various writings on government and the three tracts of 1525 to discover this consistency. Revolt was far worse than murder or any other great crime against the State. The only way that revolt could be met was by stern and prompt action by the government. It was the government's duty, not just its right, to attack the rebels at the earliest possible opportunity and to destroy this cancer which was infecting the entire land and which was killing innocent people and depriving them of their land and livelihood.

Thus a clearly defined trend in Luther's thinking on revolt was evident for all to see over three years before the Peasants' War, evident from his previous actions, and certainly discernible from his numerous writings. Even though the Wittenberg affair and the Knights' Revolt were small and perhaps even unimportant in comparison to the Peasants' War, they give an excellent sample of Luther's actions in case of a future and greater uprising.

In discussing Luther's political theories it was evident that Luther was essentially conservative in political and governmental matters. To him government, secular government, was a divine institution, ordained by God to rule on earth for the protection, welfare, and prosperity of the subjects. It was the government's responsibility to wield the temporal sword to punish wrongdoers. And the government must punish as well as protect. It must not be too strict, because as Luther said, moderation was better since it is better to save the innocent than be guilty of punishing the guilty unjustly. And too it would be better to allow a knave to go free from punishment in doubtful cases rather than bring harm on a good man because the world has too many knaves and too few good men. Luther's advice to people everywhere was to obey the rulers in all things. If there existed a doubt as to the emperor's power or if there was a doubt as to the prince's right to compel obedience in certain instances, the subject should obey anyway. The individual then could never be accused of disobedience or rebellion against his lawful lord. Luther's opinion of secular government was essentially medieval in character, but he did believe that the secular government had the right to initiate ecclesiastical reform if the members of the spiritual estate did not carry out the necessary reform. This was placing in the hands of secular rulers a tremendous amount of power which could and did eventually lead to state control over the churches in large parts of Germany, particularly in the north.[1]

Luther's ideal government was a type of limited monarchy as instituted in the Holy Roman Empire. He would support another type if that should arise. He said that the form of government was up to human determination. The ruler should be the first servant of the state. He should be a type of father for his subjects, and he should not rely too heavily on the advice and wisdom of his counselors. The requisites for ruling were severe, and he readily admitted that only a few princes could possibly qualify as real and true Christian rulers. He said that Christian rulers were few and far between. But he was establishing an ideal, and at least he set a pattern which princes might follow or attempt to emulate.

But Luther was also conservative in economic and social matters. The best occupation for the people was agriculture. He was opposed to the undue emphasis (his own estimation) which had been placed on commerce and manufacturing. This had resulted in Germany to the search for luxury and material things which had led ultimately to greed and avarice. He cited the Children of Israel as examples of a people who had concentrated on agriculture: farming and keeping of flocks. These were the occupations which God had considered the best, and he allowed the Children of Israel to flourish as long as they concentrated on these occupations. Other peoples had emphasized trade, and where were they now?

Socially and economically Luther was a member of that rising middle class which was to play such an important role in Europe's history. He was not a wealthy man in the sense of the Fuggers or Medicis nor could he rival the wealth of the princes or such a man as Franz von Sickingen. Most of Luther's wealth was tied up in real estate and in donations given to him by members of the nobility and other interested persons. And most of these had been given to him after his marriage to Katie. But his holdings did give him a great stake in the status quo, and anything that arose which would endanger this wealth was sure to

cause concern for the reformer. His parents too were members of
that same middle class. And yet he could be and was identified
with the farmers. It was only natural that they would look to
him for aid and moral support. After all he too had had a humble
beginning. His parents had originally been farmers, and had had
to struggle for a living. His grandparents were farmers, tillers of
the soil.

As mentioned before, Luther's actions during the war have
been severely criticized by his opponents. Just what were these
actions which have caused such comment? First, he took a trip
throughout portions of Germany, to inspect firsthand some of the
results of the peasant uprising. Ostensibly he was to be on hand
for the opening of a new school in Eisleben. In April, 1525, he
used this trip as an occasion to make a personal inspection. He
had received many reports about peasant activity; now he could
see for himself. On the journey he stopped at Borna, and here he
delivered a sermon meant to still and quiet the unrest in that
area. The sermon did not have the desired results. He experienced hecklers in the audience which made the delivery of the
sermon difficult. He was learning firsthand the seriousness of
the movement.

Luther had also been sent a copy of the Twelve Articles, and
he had written a reply. It was a moderate tract, and nothing in
this piece of writing of the Reformer has caused a great deal of
criticism, except that some have discovered an inconsistency. In
the first part, Luther blames the princes for being the cause of the
revolt. In the second, he commiserates with the peasants but says
that they should not revolt. There is no inconsistency present.
Luther is merely being nice to the peasants, sympathizing with
them but also admonishing them against force and violence.
Tracts Two and Three have been severely condemned. But even
here Luther merely repeats what he has said so many times previously about the evils of rebellion and about his support in all
cases of the legally established government.

A third action was his marriage to Katherine von Bora. This
was considered inopportune, but actually Luther was using it as
a means of defiance and a challenge to the papal authorities.

And he was also demonstrating to his supporters that he was willing to take this serious and irrevocable step in the belief that his movement would succeed. What would have been the fate of Luther if his movement had failed, and he had been turned over to the imperial authorities for punishment once the "Evangelical Movement" collapsed? A heretic, a blasphemer, and a renegade monk who had married an escaped nun, would have been among the charges against him. But in June 1525, he was throwing a challenge in the face of the Romanists.

Other than his marriage was there anything present in Luther's actions or words which differed in any respect from his actions in 1522 and 1523? The answer is no. The use of the word consistency becomes almost monotonous in its regularity. But the three uprisings form a pattern of behavior for Luther, a pattern which he never changed. These three revolts form a block of events which may be studied to demonstrate the fortitude and courage of the Reformer.

What are some of the reasons why Luther was successful in quieting and stopping the uprising in Wittenberg in 1522 and was so unsuccessful in 1525? First of all, the revolt of 1522 was local in character and rather weak in number of adherents. Wittenberg was only one among many smaller cities throughout Germany, and it was the first to really feel the effects of the Reformation, since it was the headquarters and home of the leader of the reform movement. Only a few people were involved in these early disturbances. Besides Karlstadt and Zwilling there were no leaders to cope with. These two men plus the arrival of the Zwickau Prophets, a rather peculiar sect, had inaugurated the reforms, and had also led the people to violence and disorder. As was seen, Luther at first reports was unconcerned, believing that the disturbances were in the nature of student pranks, and having been a faculty member for some years, he was quite accustomed to such goings-on. Once, however, the seriousness of the affair became apparent, he took rather drastic measures. He gave up his place of safety and refuge at the Wartburg and returned to Wittenberg in order to resume personal leadership. Philip Melanchthon, his trusted lieutenant in his absence, had been unable to stop the property destruction and radical changes in the church service which had been started particularly by Karlstadt and Zwilling. He had failed to cope with the leaders of the rioters; he seemed to be unsure of himself at this moment of crisis and incapable of stemming the tide of radicalism.

With the return of Luther, however, the entire uprising fell flat. Here Luther was most brilliant. Nowhere before or since were his words so effective before his congregation. It must have been an awe-inspiring sight for the members of the congregation to see before them once more this brave and courageous man who had stood before the great princes of the empire and had refused to recant or change one whit of his writings until and unless they had been proved wrong by the Scriptures. In eight short sermons, preached on consecutive days, Luther stilled the voices of revolt, and brought once more quiet and peace to the streets of Wittenberg. No longer was the City Council to fear that Town property would be destroyed by the wantonness of a group of wild-eyed radicals. In the sermons Luther cajoled, scolded, and verbally chastized the people sitting before him in the congregation for not having love in their hearts for their fellow men. Luther knew that they had been taught the Gospel. He could not criticize the preaching. But the fruit of that teaching, Love, was missing. He asked them why they hadn't come to him for advice, or contacted him for counsel. He was not so far away that he would not have been able to aid them. But no, they had gone their own way, and through violence, destruction of property, and coercion of their fellow citizens, they had forced through reforms which in most instances were a matter of free choice for the individual. Luther acted as a disapproving parent toward erring children. He was successful. Zwilling confessed to his wrongs, and Karlstadt was forced to quiet down. No longer were the Zwickau Prophets to invade Wittenberg, and cause so much consternation among the learned scholars of the university. Luther was rewarded by the City Council with magnificent gifts for his success.

The revolt of 1525 was too great in extent for anyone to stop singlehanded as had been done in 1522. He had travelled to see for himself the extent and seriousness of the new uprising. The movement had progressed too far by April, 1525, for even Luther's mighty voice to have much effect. The radical leaders of the peasantry had drawn too glamorous a picture for the poor and unlearned, and the passionate speeches inflamed them to a point where only violent action by them would satisfy their hunger for action and change. The greater numbers and the larger area involved in 1525 was a block for Luther. True, he exhorted his followers to preach against the uprising wherever they were, but it was too late, and even some of the pastors were rather cool to stopping the peasants in their demands and their attempts to improve their lot.

Now one can ask an important question and one which Luther must have asked himself many times during the course of the Peasants' War: What would he gain by a peasant victory, and what would he gain by a princely victory? In answering these two questions he would determine to a great extent his own course of actions. In April, 1525, after having received a copy of the Twelve Articles, Luther made a quick trip to Eisleben in order to be present at the opening of the new school. On this journey he had several remarkable experiences. First he had some conversations with people who had had firsthand experiences of peasant atrocities and destruction in the neighborhood. These reports alone were enough to convince the Reformer that the peasants erred in their actions. Second, Luther saw for himself some of the devastated areas, and the destruction was pointed out as having been caused by bands of roving peasants who destroyed merely for the love of destruction. Third, he had preached at Borna and in the midst of the sermon he had had the remarkable experience of hearing hecklers in the audience so that the sermon was difficult to present and even more difficult for the interested to hear. It is possible and probable that the hecklers were followers of some of the radicals among the peasants. But even so Luther was actually interrupted several times during the course of the sermon.

On the basis of his own personal observations and experiences, then, Luther was able to evaluate the movement and come to a decision. He was primarily afraid for the success of his own movement; not for his life or property. What chance of success was there for the new Evangel if such radicals as those who had appeared in Borna were to take charge or be responsible for the movement in a particular locale? Luther was conservative, and he wanted no wide-eyed radicals in his movement. He had seen what radicals could do in Wittenberg three years previously. And the experience at Wittenberg convinced him that a Reformation through force could only bring discredit and harm to him and his movement, and particularly it would bring shame and dishonor to the Gospel itself. A Reformation was impossible through violent means.

From purely economic interests, as a man of the middle class, it was only natural that Luther could presume that he would lose greatly if the peasants were successful. The peasants had destroyed much property in their pillaging, and would the lands and holdings of Luther be more exempt from this destruction than others of his class? How would he fare in case the peasants moved to the environs of Wittenberg? What would happen to the Black Cloister and the property of his own immediate family? Also what would happen to the existing government which he had supported so vehemently and ardently throughout his entire career? The peasants had talked about the abolition of serfdom and the equality of all men. It is tue that the Twelve Articles contained no clear-cut political program; but reports of "No Lord but the Emperor" had reached him, and this was contrary to all that he believed concerning political affairs.

No, Peasant Victory would bring chaos, and there would be no end to the bloodshed and violence. The peasants would not bring order or prosperity to Germany. The land would suffer through lack of cultivation (this was already happening); the economy would suffer as a result. In his own mind Luther could see nothing good coming from a peasant victory. Had the peasants demonstrated in any of their actions a reasonableness and willingness to accept guidance and advice from anyone? In the spring of 1525, they had, but apparently, this was a sham, and he came to believe that they never meant to take seriously the advice which he had given in his reply to the Twelve Articles. When there had been a chance to return to their farms peacefully, they had refused. They had committed such atrocities as the Weinsberg affair. The peasants should not win. Everything must be done to stop them.

With the above reply to his question about the peasants, Luther naturally examined the princes. Here were the legally constituted authorities, ordained by God to rule on earth, to protect the people, to wield the temporal sword for the safety and prosperity of all. This alone would have assured the support of Luther for the Princes. But there were also other considerations. Gratitude to the House of Saxony (Frederick the Wise and his successors) for the protection and aid which it had extended to him ever since he came into the spotlight of controversy. It had shielded him from the imperial authorities and from the papists; it had given him tremendous economic aid and frank moral support in his efforts to bring about a reformation. His movement had prospered under the House of Saxony; Frederick the Wise had been a prudent man, and it is true that he retained his relics and images and never formally embraced the religion of his most famous subject. Yet the "Evangelical Movement" had grown, and had been secure. Wittenberg had become the center of a widening and ever-expanding movement. And of the reasons for this, one of the most important was Frederick of Saxony and other German princes who had become Protestants.

Also Luther believed in a stable form of government. The peasants did not. The philosophies of government were diametrically opposite. If the princes won over the peasants in the war, Luther could assume continued support by members of the nobility for the Evangel. All of the signs pointed to this. The big factor in considering the advantages and disadvantages for a princely or a peasant victory was not what would be the effects on Luther personally, on his property holdings, even on his family. But the principal factor was the effect on the Gospel, and the freedom of the movement to expand and grow. In the peasant camp there were such rabid radicals as Münzer, who thoroughly hated Luther. Men like Münzer were making the freedom of the

Christian into a carnal thing, something of the flesh. They were distorting the Gospel, and bringing disrepute and harm to the Word of God. They were worse than mere rebels. Because they combined rebellion with a violation of God Himself. This was an evil which must be stamped out. They might hate him and call him the servant of the princes. That was all right. He was the servant of the princes. That was the ordinance of God.

Now it is necessary to ask the question, how justified are Luther's critics who criticized him so vehemently at the time and who since have condemned him for his actions during the war?[2] First of all, What are some of the actions which have been condemned? There are four basic criticisms:

1. He used intemperate language in the three tracts written during the war.

2. His unfortunate timing of the publication of these tracts, showed poor judgment.

3. He had given the peasants cause to believe that he was in favor or sympathetic with their movement, and then in a sudden turnabout, he went against them.

4. His marriage to Katherine von Bora was a gross error. Let us examine each of these in turn and determine if possible if the critics are justified.

Concerning Luther's language used in three tracts written as a result of the peasant revolt, his critics as well as his defenders have used three arguments:

a. His language was intemperate and violent, and there was no excuse for this language coming from a scholarly man like Luther.

b. Although the language was imprudent, Luther was provoked by attacks on him and by circumstances to use such words, and therefore, there are mitigating factors present.

c. His language was no different from that of others of the 16th century.

In assessing the above arguments, the third one has far more validity than the others, and actually explains fairly well Luther's vocabulary. If one examines the writings of other scholars of the 16th century, whether they be Luther critics, defenders, or neutralists, it is apparent that it was common for a man to use rather colorful vocabulary in his published material. Eck, Emser, and Erasmus were certainly not exempt from using what might be considered even vituperative language. Luther was thus no different from his contemporaries. If he is to be judged, it must be done on the basis of the 16th and not later centuries when certain refinements entered the picture.

Far more biting has been the charge that the timing of his tracts was unfortunate. This has been applied particularly to the publication of the second tract, *Against the Murdering and Thieving Bands of Peasants*. The ardent critics point out that the peasants had already suffered a decisive defeat at the Battle of Frankenhausen in May, 1525, and that the tract appeared in June, over a month later. (It probably was published at the end of May.) That the tract in effect was calling for the princes to slay and stab defenseless men who already had been defeated, and who were facing their opponents empty-handed, and who wished for nothing but peace. However, one has to review the Peasants' War, and understand that the word "war" is really incorrect. It was a revolt; there was no coordination among the numerous peasant groups; no general staff to direct and plan operations; and certainly no concerted or united plan for operations against the princes. When the defeat of the group at Frankenhausen occurred, there were still large groups elsewhere in Germany, which were still fighting and still causing considerable difficulty for the authorities. So no one single battle put a definite end to the peasant movement. Frankenhausen was the greatest single battle; more peasants were slain here than in any other battle. It did signify quite clearly that the peasants could not possibly win; that the lords would gain the upper hand. The peasants actually were defeated in a series of campaigns, some of them minor in terms of participants, others large, such as Frankenhausen. However, even if the criticism is allowed to stand, can Luther be blamed for a delay in publication? He had actually begun work on this second tract before the battle of Frankenhausen. And the manuscript was in the hands of the printers before Luther received news of the peasant defeat. He allowed it to be printed in fact as a lesson to the remaining rebels in hopes that it would have some influence in preventing the other groups from their rebellion. The fact that it did appear after the battle, and that it seemed ill-timed, is of little importance. It is not a just criticism of Luther, though he was shocked and angered by reports of peasant atrocities. The work at Weinsberg was horrifying, and when he received news of Rohrbach's execution, he in effect said it was a good thing. Also he was in a sense pleased with the demise of Thomas Münzer, who was executed after Frankenhausen. This was the very end which he had predicted for all the rebels. It was merely justifying his own beliefs and vindication that God would act against the seditioners.

One of the most damning of all criticisms, however, was the one concerning his aid and support for the peasants in the early months of 1525. The peasants had considered Luther one of the few men in Germany capable and just enough to comment on the program embodied in the Twelve Articles. His comment did give some cause for hope that he was on their side. It is true that he vehemently condemned the nobles. And he said that the princes, ecclesiastical and secular, were really responsible for the evils present and for the abuses against which the peasantry were agitating. If the nobles had acted in a wise and Christian manner and treated their subjects fairly and according to God's Commandments, there would never have been a peasant uprising. But he also admonished the peasants for taking matters into their own hands. They had no right to use force against the secular rulers. Luther even went so far as to say that he would not comment on the majority of the Articles since these involved legal questions, and he was not competent to judge such matters. Did he make any sudden turnabout? The answer is, of course, no. Nowhere in his writings, speeches, or letters can one find a shred of support for the theory that he had given the peasants cause for a belief that he would help them against the princes. On the contrary, he had written thousands of words on the very opposite proposition. As noted before, rebellion was the worst evil that could be visited on man. And he stated categorically that he would always support the legally constituted authorities, regardless of the cause of the rebels or whether their cause might be fair. It was *never* right in his opinion, which he expressed so eloquently, to rebel against the government.

But the critics point out that Luther's writings contained the germ of revolt. Look at the titles of the various tracts on political matters: *Freedom of the Christian; On Secular Authority, How Far One Should Obey It; An Address to the Christian Nobility of the German Nation Concerning Reform.* It is true that the titles could and did lead many to believe that Luther would favor the abolition of serfdom; that all men were equal in the political and economic spheres. But Luther did not say these things. Can he be criticized for the interpretation which others put on his writings or what unlearned men and radicals told the people concerning what he was preaching? True, many Lutheran pastors, far from Wittenberg, had a tremendous influence on their parishioners. And some did inflame the people with their ideas of Christian freedom and liberty. Many were turning a belief in the Gospel and a freedom to believe into a carnal and worldly concept. Luther did not do this. If criticism is justified, then that criticism should be directed against the titles of his various tracts and not against the contents. "The Christian Freedom of all, the equality of high and low in the common priesthood was proclaimed in the most incautious and seductive terms."[3] In reality, then, Luther is being criticized for the titles and not the contents, and for the actions of some of his followers rather than for his own actions. In defense of Luther, he should not be held responsible for the work, actions, and utterances of every Lutheran pastor and every follower of the "Evangelical Movement" that wandered throughout Europe, proclaiming to the people the message of the Gospel as interpreted by themselves to suit their own fancies.

Actually Luther had not given the peasants or any other group cause to believe that he would support them in an uprising against the government. It was ridiculous and farthest from his mind, and it was contrary to all that he believed.

A valuable synopsis of the whole situation has been presented by Professor D. Heinrich Bornkamm at Heidelberg. In his most recent book on Luther (1958), he made this remark: "During the Peasant Revolt (1525) his principle was put to the severest test. Social and religious demands were woven into a program of the revolt; Christian liberty was its sublimest idea . . . He strenuously opposed the idea of a rebellion invoked in the name of Christ, even staking his life in the issue . . . He had no choice but to encourage and support the government in its conflict with the wild hordes incited by fanatical instigators like Münzer." Bornkamm also called Karlstadt and Münzer "mystic fanatics." He argued that it is absurd to brand Luther "as the father of the revolution. After all, whom did Münzer and the other factious spirits hate more than him?"[4]

Important is Luther's letter of May 30, 1525, addressed to Rühel. He says: "Well, he who has seen Münzer may say that he has seen the devil in the flesh, filled with anger. O Lord, when there is such a spirit in the farmers, it is high time that they be killed like mad dogs. For the devil apparently sees the last days near, and he wants to stir the soup and set forth all the hellish power."[5]

Schwiebert, like Bainton, is inclined to exonerate the *Schwärmer*. He says: "In recent years considerable investigation has been made regarding the religious and social teaching of the radical groups which Luther described as the 'Schwaermer.' These Studies reveal that many of them were laymen, simple uneducated folk, and that Luther judged them superficially and unfairly . . . Karlstadt and Thomas Münzer may be said to have represented the two extreme wings of radicalism, but there were dozens of other leaders, among them Schappler, Hubmaier, Waibel, Storch, each with his following."[6] He supports Lilje and Bornkamm and Gerdes in their condemnation of Münzer. Luther was not superficially condemning the people whom he called the *Schwärmer*. On the contrary, he spoke and wrote with a full understanding of their confused ideas in the field of politics and religion.

Again, timing is involved in the criticism of his marriage. It was considered inopportune to marry Katie in the midst of the revolt; to celebrate his marriage just after news was received of the slaughter at Frankenhausen. Actually, many of Luther's own followers were far more critical of Luther's marriage than his opponents. They wanted him to marry someone of wealth and social position. Katie had neither. Luther was defying all his opponents and carrying through an idea and belief which he had long espoused.

There is no denying the fact that the war had a tremendous influence on Martin Luther. He had come from a family of the Middle Class. Even though Hans Luther had not been a peasant, the life and occupation of the peasant was not far in the background. It had not been so long before that the relatives of Luther had themselves been simple tillers of the soil. And Martin did feel a kinship and a certain identity with the peasantry of Germany. He was not a member of the nobility nor was he a very wealthy man. In an earlier chapter, Luther's wealth was investigated and discovered that he and his parents had accumulated a considerable fortune, but it in no way compared with the wealth of the Fuggers or the other great banking and commercial families of Europe. Luther considered himself a man of simplicity, having much in common with the peasantry. Also he had an abiding faith in the simple farmer. The tillers of the soil were doing God's work. Luther favored agricultural pursuits as the best occupation in which man could become engaged. He was considerably distressed by these farmers when they arose in revolt against their lords and attempted to bring about change by violent means. Likewise, he was disturbed by the naiveté of these people in the ease with which they were led by a few radicals. One of the most serious results of the war for Luther personally was that he lost faith in the common man. He had seen the common man give vent to his passions: looting, pillaging and destroying property and lives; actions which in no way could he approve and actions which had to be stopped at all costs. Losing faith, however, does not imply that he had ever considered the peasantry capable of governing themselves. On the contrary, political equality was anathema to Luther. But the people had demonstrated that they needed more than ever the secular authority, and this authority should be strict and must punish rebels very severely.

The war also had the unfortunate result of fostering radicalism within the "Evangelical Movement." The defeat of Frankenhausen and Königshafen did not eliminate the radical leaders for all time. It is true that Münzer was out of the picture and that Karlstadt had been effectively silenced. But the radicals who had made their appearance during the Peasants' War were not all like Münzer and Karlstadt. In the place of Münzer came the Anabaptists and the so-called Sacramentarians. The city of Strasburg turned against Wittenberg, but it also broke more firmly with Rome than Wittenberg had done thus far. After the year 1525, Protestantism did not get checked as far as many historians have concluded. On the contrary, both Lutheranism and Calvinism made enormous advances, especially in those areas where the leadership in modern times would be concentrated.

It has been generally believed that the masses of the people lost faith in Luther. On the contrary, the lower classes in Germany, England, and the Dutch Republic liked his views on the powers of the civil rulers. They wanted above all things peace and order. In their inner hearts they liked to worship heroes, the kind that would be like Luther, not the men like Alva who came to the Netherlands in order to suppress local liberties. Switzerland and the Netherlands were attracted by the political and economic views of Luther, whose opinions Calvin made more popular. The English people in particular favored Luther's works dealing with the liberty of the Christian. Luther had a famous home where untold numbers of political leaders were lavishly entertained, and where they could all see his wife at work among the students.

Luther himself was not changed much by that war. He was shocked by the behaviour of the unruly farmers, but he was just as shocked later on by the evil deeds of several princes. Here is his testimony: "Drunkenness has spread among our youth so that now the greater part of the finest, most talented young men (especially among the Nobles and at the Court) undermine their health, their body, and their life . . . before the time . . . Men are now avaricious, unmerciful, impure, insolent . . . than formerly under the Pope." He remembered, he said, that when he was young a nobleman was ashamed of his immorality. But the whole trouble was that he had not known much about those nobles before the year 1520. Gradually he became better acquainted with them, and near the end of his life he had to go to Mansfeld in order to settle a quarrel between two princes.[7]

It would seem, therefore, that the idea of many biographers to the effect that Luther favored the princes against the emperor is not based upon a careful study of the original sources. Luther was extremely reluctant to built up the powers of the local princes at the expense of the emperor. It was only when the latter broke his contract with the princes that they might rise against him with court measures or armed forces.

On May 3, 1525, Luther was in the town of Weimar, which was made world-famous by Goethe and his colleagues, and for which reason Luther's works were published in the great Weimar Edition. He had gone to his native country, the region around Mansfeld and Eisleben, to see just what the rebellious farmers had been doing. He wrote a letter to Frederick Myconius, who was to become one of the leaders in the building of the Lutheran Church. In the fifth volume of his great edition of Luther's letters, Ernst Ludwig Enders made this remark at the end of this letter: "After Luther had observed that his treatise entitled, *A Warning for Peace*, had remained without effect, he tried to obtain a peaceful solution through a personal intervention, starting at Eisleben. On April 23 he had been in Weimar, and then went to Orlamunde, Jena, Eisleben, and Nordhausen, returning on May 2nd to Weimar. The result he had was indicated in a letter written on May 1st by Hans Zeysz to the Elector: 'Doctor Luther is in the Mansfeld county, but he is unable to put down the uprising there.' "[8] Luther wrote in his second pamphlet that he had made a personal inspection in Thuringia, which was Electoral Saxony to a great extent: "People know that the farmers in Franconia intended to do nothing but rob, burn, destroy, and ruin, out of sheer mischief. The Thuringian farmers I have watched myself, and the more one admonishes and teaches them the more obstreperous, proud, and mad they become."[9]

The years from 1521 to 1525 may be called the years of crisis, the critical years, or the testing years. Any of these descriptive phrases would be reasonably accurate. These years produced two trends which were to be of great importance to both Luther and to the reform movement which he headed. First, it was evident that the reform movement was to be fragmented. It was in this period that many, many other reformers appeared on the scene to preach reform of the church. And this resulted in the establishment of many new churches throughout Europe. Secondly, it also became evident that by 1525 Luther was no longer the recognized leader of the reform movement. Others had appeared on the scene to provide competition for the Saxon reformer. Thus fragmentation and loss of leadership were two of the immediate results of these critical, testing years.

It should be stated, however, that Luther was not necessarily responsible for these trends. It is debatable whether he had the authority or prestige to stop the fragmentation or to be recognized as leader throughout Europe. Certainly his prestige and reputation were not seriously damaged by any of the three movements which have been examined. Luther exercised a considerable influence on Zwingli, Calvin, Cranmer and many other reformers who later were to be called Protestant. Whether Luther could have reduced the influence of the radicals (the Schwaermer) is highly doubtful. And it is just as debatable whether he wanted such leadership.

By 1525 the Evangelical Movement in the Holy Roman Empire was in full swing. Both the authorities at Rome and the emperor had waited too long to take action against Luther and his colleagues. The reformation would continue. Even the disasters of the Peasants' War were not great enough to stop the reformation or for that matter even to slow it down. The pace would quicken. New trends, new results, would appear.

NOTES

ABBREVIATIONS

W. A.   Weimar Edition of Luther's Works.
E. A.   Erlangen Edition of Luther's Works.
P. E.   Philadelphia Edition of Luther's Works.
A. E.   American Edition of Luther's Works.
Bainton.   Roland H. Bainton, *Here I Stand.*
Schwiebert.   Ernst G. Schwiebert, *Luther and His Times.*
Hyma.   Albert Hyma, *Renaissance to Reformation.*
W. B.   *D. Martin Luther's Briefwechsel.*
W. T.   Tischreden.

CHAPTER ONE

1. Schwiebert, *Luther and His Times,* p. 513. See also W. T. Tischreden, V, p. 82.
2. Preserved Smith and Charles M. Jacobs (eds.), *Luther's Correspondence and Other Contemporary Letters,* 2 vols., Philadelphia: 1913-1918, II, pp. 28-29.
3. W. B. Briefwechsel, II, p. 445.
4. P. E., p. 387. E. Gordon Rupp has an delightful short essay in *Luther Today,* pp. 107-128, on "Luther and Carlstadt." Although the author is not particularly kind to Carlstadt, he presents a vivid picture of this unstable man whose actions in 1521 and 1522 helped to estrange Luther from him. Later events during the Peasants' War were to cause a complete break between the two.
5. P. E., II, p. 388.
6. Hermann Barge, *Andreas Bodenstein von Karlstadt,* 2 vols., Leipzig, 1905, I, pp. 290-291.
7. Luther held no grudges against Zwilling. Following the Wittenberg disturbances in 1522, Luther personally recommended him for appointment as pastor and superintendant at Torgau. Georg Berbig, *Georg Spalatin und sein Verhättnis zu Martin Luther auf Grund ihres Briefwechsels bis zum Jahre 1525,* Halle, 1906, p. 188.

8. John Oyer's excellent monograph, *Lutheran Reformers Against Anabaptists*, The Hague, 1964, has an excellent chapter on this subject: "The Schwärmer, Luther, and Melanchthon," pp. 6-40.

9. P. E., II, p. 388.

10. A. L. Richter (ed.), *Die Evangelischen Kirchenordnungen des Sechzehnten Jahrhunderts*, 2 vols., Weimar, 1846, II, pp. 484-485. (See Appendix A.)

11. The text of the preface can be examined in A. E., vol. 45, *The Christian in Society*, II, pp. 161-176.

12. Luther to Spalatin, 17 January 1522 in A. Hyma, *Luther's Theological Development from Erfure to Worms*, New York, 1928, p. 72.

13. Luther to Wenceslaus Link, 19 March 1522, *Luther's Theological Development from Erfure to Worms*, p. 72.

14. This translation may be found in Roland H. Bainton, *Here I Stand: A Life of Martin Luther*, New York, 1950, p. 212. (See also W. B., II, pp. 454-455.)

15. In the Introduction to volume 51 (Sermons I) of the American Edition (A. E.), the editor gives an excellent survey of Luther's sermons, how they were composed, the transcriber, etc. The Weimar Edition contains some 2000 sermons with a detailed index in volume 22. Luther usually spoke only from brief notes. Some of his sermons were later rewritten by him for publication while others came to us from shorthand notes taken by listeners in the audience.

16. P. E., II, p. 389.

17. P. E., II, pp. 391-396; A. E., LI, pp. 70-75.

18. P. E., II, pp. 393; A. E., LI, p. 72.

19. P. E., II, pp. 395-397; A. E., LI, pp. 74-76.

20. A. E., LI, p. 77; P. E., II, p. 399-400.

21. P. E., II, p. 415; A. E., LI, p. 91.

22. P. E., II, p. 418; A. E., LI, p. 94.

23. This statement could have referred to the Elector of Saxony who donated thousands of sacred relics to the churches of electoral Saxony. To his dying day Frederick was very proud of this collection and the indulgences connected with them. Vast sums had also been spent on the beautiful cases which protected these relics.

CHAPTER TWO

1. Preserved Smith, *The Age of the Reformation*, New York, 1920, p. 83.

2. Two works are of particular importance for an understanding of Hutten and Sickingen. These are Hajo Holborn, *Ulrich von Hutten*, Leipzig, 1929. Translated by Roland H. Bainton, *Ulrich von Hutten and the German*

Reformation, New Haven, 1937, and William R. Hitchcock, *The Background of the Knights' Revolt 1522-1523,* Berkeley and Los Angeles, 1958.

3. Although this change to humanism is particularly important in the life of Hutten, it is outside the scope of this study to do more than mention it. Holborn's book already cited gives a good account of this aspect of Hutten's career.

4. Hajo Holborn, *Ulrich von Hutten,* New Haven, 1937, p. 111.

5. *Ibid.*

6. For an excellent photograph of the ruins of the Ebernburg which clearly shows its formidable defensive position, see the album of plates in Ernst G. Schwiebert, *Luther and His Times,* St. Louis, 1950, Plate LXII.

7. In his fine book already cited, William R. Hitchcock presents a very interesting picture of the Knightly class during the early Reformation. He points out that some of the knights would appear to have more basis for supporting the Roman Catholic Church than the new evangelical since territorial princes like Philip of Hesse took such revenge on the Knights during and after the revolt. Also there was a question involving legal status. Some of the Knights enjoyed immediacy (no lord but the emperor), confiscation of Knight's property by the prince was questionable. If politics alone were considered, the Knights should have supported Charles V. Instead, these men supported Luther and remained staunchly loyal to the reform movement. In spite of persecution in 1523 and 1524, they were pro-Luther.

8. Holborn, p. 194.

9. Schwiebert, *Luther and His Times,* St. Louis, 1950, p. 487.

10. Enders, *Luthers Briefwechsel,* IV, p. 40.

11. *Ibid.,* p. 143.

12. P. Smith, p. 83.

13. R. H. Fife, *The Revolt of Martin Luther,* New York, 1957, p. 618.

CHAPTER THREE

1. Schwiebert, *Luther and His Times,* St. Louis, 1950, p. 556.

2. As was shown in Chapter Two, the Knightly class held similar attitudes toward the burghers and merchant class. Their resentment of these classes had substantially the same basis as did peasant resentment.

3. Jacob Salwyn Schapiro, "Social Reform and the Reformation" in studies in History, Economics, and Public Law, XXXIV, No. 2, New York, 1909, p. 64.

4. Thomas Lindsay, *A History of the Reformation,* 2 vols., New York, 1906-07, I, p. 97.

5. Roy Pascal, *The Social Basis of the German Reformation,* London, 1933, p. 129.

6. Schwiebert, *Luther and His Times,* St. Louis, 1950, pp. 556-560.
7. *Ibid.,* p. 558.
8. *Ibid.,* p. 560.
9. Pascal, pp. 129-131.

CHAPTER FOUR

1. For a brief discussion of the literature concerning the Peasants' War see Robert N. Crossley, "The Peasants' War in Germany: Some Observations on Recent Historiography" in *Essays on Luther,* ed. by Kenneth A. Strand, Ann Arbor, 1969.

2. Schwiebert, *Luther and His Times,* St. Louis, 1950, p. 562.

3. Hermann J. Weigand, "A Close-up of the German Peasants' War," in Connecticut Academy of Arts and Sciences, *Transactions,* XXXV, 1944, pp. 1-32. The full documented account is found in Vol. CXXXIX of the Bibliothek des Literarisches verein in Stuttgart.

4. The original manuscript is preserved in the city archives of the Town of Rothenburg, but in 1888 it was published in the series at Stuttgart. This is one of the most important sources for the study of the role of a city in the war.

5. Numerous copies of these articles are available in English translation: B. J. Kidd, ed., *Documents Illustrative of the Continental Reformation,* Oxford, 1911, pp. 174-179 and P. E., IV, pp. 210-216 are two readily available translations.

6. The most recent and most helpful biography of this strange man is Eric W. Gritsch, *Reformer Without a Church. Thomas Muentzer,* Philadelphia, 1967. Again the historiographical article in *Essays on Luther* would also be helpful.

7. E. Gordon Rupp has a delightful essay on Karlstadt and his relations with Luther in "Luther and Carlstadt," in *Luther Today,* Decorah, Iowa, 1957, pp. 107-128. This is one of the volumes in the Luther Lecture Series, a fine contribution to our knowledge of Luther.

8. Brief sketches in the Histories of the Peasants' War provide the meager information on the military leaders among the Peasants. See Bax and G. Franz.

9. The chapter on the Knights' Revolt adequately covers the changes in Europe which caused unrest among the Knightly class.

CHAPTER FIVE

1. For other demands or other articles see Günther Franz, *Quellen zur Geschichte des Bauernkrieges,* München, 1963. The lack of unity and or-

ganization in the Peasants' War is nowhere more evident than in the numerous lists, each one drafted and accepted by only one or a few peasant groups.

2. W. A., XVIII, pp. 291-334; A. E., Vol., 46, pp. 17-43; P.E., Vol. IV, pp. 219-244. Extensive quotations and commentaries on this tract also appear in A. Hyma, *Renaissance to Reformation,* Grand Rapids, 1955 and in H. Bornkamm, *Luther's World of Thought,* St. Louis, 1958.

3. Numerous copies of the Twelve Articles are available. I have consulted the Philadelphia Edition of Luther's Works, Vol. IV, pp. 210-216, and the copy in B. J. Kidd, *Documents Illustrative of the Continental Reformation,* Oxford, 1911, reprinted 1967, pp. 174-179.

4. This subject has been adequately treated by Ernest G. Schwiebert, *Luther and His Times. The Reformation from a New Perspective* (St. Louis, 1950), p. 564.

5. Luther to John Rühel at Mansfeld, Seeburg, May 4, 1525, in P. Smith and C. M. Jacobs, (eds.) *Luther's Correspondence and Other Contemporary Letters,* 2 vols., Philadelphia, 1913, I, pp. 308-310. (See also W. A. Briefwechsel, III, pp. 479-482.)

6. A. E., 46, pp. 49-55; P. E., IV, pp. 248-254; W. A., XVIII, 357-361.

7. As long as Luther had been studying documents like the *Twelve Articles,* he could retain a calm perspective. This can be seen in the context of some recent articles on the Peasants' War: (1) Ernst Walder, "Politischen Gehalt der 12 Artikel der deutschen Bauerschaft von 1525," in *Schweizer Beiträge zur allgeinen Geschihte,* XII, 1954, pp. 5-23; (2) Friedrich Pietsch, "Die Artikel der Limpurger Bauern," in *Zeitschrift für württembergische Landesgeshichte,* XIII, 1954, pp. 120-149; (3) E. Lauppe, "Schwarzacher Haufen," in *Ortenau,* XXXIV, 1954, pp. 94-99; (4) Adolf Waas, "Ulrich Schmidt von Sulmingen," in *Ulm und Oberschwaben,* XXXIII, 1953, pp. 99-107. Ulrich Schmidt was one of the few peasant leaders who knew how to control his feelings, but those whom Luther heard of in the neighborhood of his own birthplace were not so well endowed with common sense. It must also be remembered that in June 1525 Luther was married, after a most exciting engagement. He was in no position to issue pamphlets on the Peasants' War that would redound to his eternal credit. His engagement and wedding have been badly distorted in some recent biographies, as indicated in Albert Hyma, *New Light on Martin Luther,* Grand Rapids, 1958, pp. 169-180, 226-231. Says Hyma: "On June 15, 1525, as we saw, Luther wrote to Rühel and two other friends at Mansfeld. He told them that his harsh booklet against the peasants had caused terrible antagonism. Everybody had turned against him, lords, clergymen, farmers; and they all wanted him destroyed. He suddenly married in the midst of all this slander and complaints against him. Would they all please attend the big banquet on June 27?" This shows that the pamphlet was not published in June but much more likely in May, contrary to certain historians.

8. W. A. Briefwechsel, III, p. 517.

9. *Ibid.*, pp. 515-516. Significant is this remark on p. 516: "Denn ich auch deste härter wider die Bauren schreibe, darumb, dass sie solche Furchtsame zu ihren Mutwillen und Gottes Strafe zwingen und nötigen, und hören nicht auf." Luther makes it quite clear that the wild peasant mobs are calling upon themselves the judgments of God and of human courts. He does not seem to be upset here, but he reasons calmly. In speaking to his own brother-in-law, who has a doctor's degree, Luther was free to discuss his own feelings and motives without getting excited.

10. This has been published many times. An excellent edition in the original language is Martin Luther, "Ein Sendbrief vom dem harten Büchlein Wider die Bauern. 1525," in *Luthers Werke in Auswahl, Unter Mitwirkung von Albert Leitzmann*, Hrsg. von Otto Clemen, 4 vols., Bonn, 1912-1913, III, pp. 75-93. See also, Albert Hyma, *Renaissance to Reformation*, Grand Rapids, 1955, pp. 326-327; and, *New Light on Martin Luther*, Grand Rapids, 1958, pp. 134-135. An admirable defense of Luther's position is found in Luther Hess Waring, *The Political Theories of Martin Luther*, New York, 1910, pp. 147-149. P. E., IV, pp. 259-281; A. E., 46, pp. 63-85.

11. Heinz Kamnitzer, *Zur Vorgeschichte des Deutschen Bauernkrieges*, Berlin, 1953.

12. Roland H. Bainton, *Here I Stand: A Life of Martin Luther*, New York, 1950, p. 277. Bainton's reasoning is similar to that of Kamnitzer in his book, pp. 119-128. The latter published the following: A. Meusel, *Thomas Müntzer und seine Zeit*, Berlin, 1952. He agrees with the opinion of Meusel.

13. Heinz Kamnitzer, *Zur Vorgeschichte des Deutschen Bauernkrieges*, Berlin, 1953, pp. 109-110. Illuminating is the following statement: "Deshalb schrieb Luther im Frühjahr: 'Fahren die Fürsten fort, auf jenes dumme Gehirn des Herzogs Georg zu hören, so befürchte ich sehr, es stehe ein Aufruhr bevor, welcher in ganz Deutschland Fürsten und Magistrate vernichten und zugleich den ganzen Klerus mit einwickeln wird.'" Duke George of Saxony, unlike the Elector Frederick of Saxony, was for years a bitter opponent of Luther and a warm friend of Erasmus. Luther saw that if he prevailed, there would indeed come forth a terrible uprising of the lower classes, which would destroy both princes and municipal magistrates. So he rallied the support of the latter against both Roman Catholic princes and men like Münzer. Having been eminently successful in 1522 and 1523, he thought in 1525 that he must be victoriuos again. To a great extent he was a victor even there.

CHAPTER SIX

1. This matter of Luther's Economic Theories has been ably expounded by Albert Hyma in his *Renaissance to Reformation*, Grand Rapids, 1955,

pp. 279-305. However, a reexamination is pertinent considering the importance of economic factors in the list of Peasant demands.

2. Heinrich Böhmer, *Der Junge Luther*, Gotha, 1925, Otto Scheel (ed.), *Martin Luther von Katholizismus zur Reformation*, Tübingen, 1921, and Ernst G. Schwiebert, *Luther and His Times. The Reformation from a New Perspective*, St. Louis, 1950, for full information on the childhood of Luther and particularly on the rise of Hans Luther in the social and economic spheres.

3. See Melanchthon's brief account in Karl Bretschneider and Heinrich Bindseil (eds.), *Corpus Reformatorum*, 97 vols., Halle, 1834-1909, *Melanchthonis Opera*, VI, 156-157; and Ernst G. Schwiebert, *Luther and His Times. The Reformation from a New Perspective*, St. Louis, 1950, pp. 99-110. See, also, Albert Hyma, *New Light on Martin Luther*, Grand Rapids, 1958, pp. 9-11. It should be noted, however, that Scheel and Schwiebert do not see eye to eye on Luther's parents as living in a large home at Eisleben.

4. Ernst G. Schwiebert, *Luther and His Times. The Reformation from a New Perspective*, St. Louis, 1950, p. 107.

5. It must be noted, however, that Luther's references to peasants in later years was anything but complimentary. Even allowing for great unreliability the Table Talks give a good picture of peasants as poor dumb beasts of burden.

6. Preserved Smith, *The Age of the Reformation*, New York, 1920; and Ernst G. Schwiebert, *Luther and His Times. The Reformation from a New Perspective*, St. Louis, 1950. Schwiebert used as a source Walter Friedensburg (ed.), *Urkundenbuch der Universitat Wittenberg*, 2 vols., Magdeburg, 1926-27. It is extremely difficult to translate 16th century monetary values to modern 20th century values. Smith has used the year 1913 as a base for comparison. Such will be the case throughout this chapter.

7. Ernst G. Schwiebert, *Luther and His Times. The Reformation from a New Perspective*, p. 268.

8. Luther's Economic Theories have been ably expounded by Albert Hyma, *Renaissance to Reformation*, Grand Rapids, 1955. This section is by no means an attempt to go over the same information in the great detail which Professor Hyma has already presented. However, the importance of economic demands presented by the peasants does dictate a reexamination of Luther's own approach to many of these same problems.

9. W. A., XV, pp. 295-298.

CHAPTER SEVEN

1. Luther used the term Romanist throughout his tracts to signify those ardent champions of papal supremacy in temporal matters. See, Albert

Hyma, "Holy Roman Empire," in *Twentieth Century Encyclopedia of Religious Knowledge: An Extension of The New Schaff Herzog Encyclopedia of Religious Knowledge*, 2 vols., Grand Rapids, 1955, I, pp. 523-524; "Investiture, I, p. 570; and, "Charles V, Emperor," I, pp. 229-230.

2. For an admirable discussion of Luther's consistency after 1525 and a clear refutation of those experts who denounce Luther for inconsistency, see Albert Hyma, *Renaissance to Reformation*, Grand Rapids, 1955, pp. 306-336. For an excellent discussion of Luther and Politics see also *Luther and Culture*, George W. Forell, Harold J. Grimm, and Theodore Hoelty-Nichel, Decorah, Iowa, Luther College Press, 1960. The first section is entitled "Luther and Politics" and is written by George W. Forell, pp. 3-72.

3. Many copies and translations are available. The Philadelphia Edition (P. E.) vol. II, pp. 61-164, remains one of the best. Even the translators of the new American Edition have not been able to make many changes.

4. P. E., II, p. 66.

5. *Ibid.*, pp. 69-71.

6. *Ibid.*, p. 99.

7. *Ibid.*, pp. 100-101.

8. *Ibid.*, p. 103.

9. *Ibid.*, p. 108-110.

10. *Ibid.*, pp. 110-111.

11. *Ibid.*, pp. 149-150.

12. *Ibid.*, p. 154.

13. *Ibid.*, p. 157.

14. *Ibid.*, p. 160.

15. *A Treatise on Good Works*, P. E., I, pp. 284-285.

16. P. E., I, pp. 266-267.

17. The other two great works produced and published in 1520 are: *The Babylonian Captivity of the Church* and *The Liberty of the Christian Man*. All three may be found in any of the standard collections.

18. P. E., II, pp. 61-62.

19. *Ibid.*, III, pp. 228-273.

20. *Ibid.*, p. 236.

21. *Ibid.*, p. 239.

22. *Ibid.*, IV, pp. 103-130.

23. *Ibid.*, pp. 142-178.

CHAPTER EIGHT

1. P. E., II, pp. 354-384.

2. *Ibid.*, III, pp. 206-222.

3. *Ibid.*, pp. 211-212.

4. *Ibid.*

5. One of the most important books on the Peasants' War to appear in the last two decades is Paul Althaus, *Luther's Haltung im Bauernkrieg,* Basel, 1953. This work is particularly valuable for its analysis of Luther's tracts on the war and its treatment of agreements signed by the nobility under pressure and threats of violence.

6. P. E., IV, pp. 259-281.

7. *Ibid.,* p. 276-278.

8. *Ibid.,* III, p. 216.

9. *Ibid.,* pp. 228-273.

10. *Ibid.,* pp. 236-237.

11. *Ibid.,* p. 250.

12. *Ibid.,* pp. 251-252.

13. *Ibid.,* pp. 257-258.

14. *Ibid.,* pp. 133-200.

15. *Ibid.,* pp. 174-175.

16. See Appendix.

17. P. E., II, pp. 312-348.

18. *Ibid.,* IV, p. 240.

19. *Ibid.,* II, p. 313.

20. *Ibid.,* p. 343.

21. Albert Hyma, *New Light on Martin Luther,* Grand Rapids, Michigan, 1958, pp. 138-139.

22. Luther H. Waring, *The Political Theories of Martin Luther,* New York, 1910, p. 277. Heinrich Bornkamm in his new book, *Luther's World of Thought,* St. Louis, 1958, p. 240, says: "Luther entertained no doubt regarding the desirability of the monarchial form of government, not only because it was the order of the day but also because history convinced him of the influence and strength of the individual personality." But Bornkamm does not prove his point. He says that the electoral counselor Fabian von Feilitzsch "was better than any ever so learned professional jurist." Now this counselor was not a prince himself but merely a well-trained adviser. In certain imperial cities there were also such persons, but who could call the municipal governments of Germany forms of monarchy? They were more like republican governments. Luther accepted these as well-ordered units in his empire, ranking with duchies and counties. For example, the city of Augsburg, which he knew so well, was not a monarchy.

23. Luther Hess Waring, *The Political Theories of Martin Luther,* New York, 1910, pp. 276-277.

24. P. E., III, pp. 264-265.

25. *Ibid.,* p. 266.

26. *Ibid.,* p. 268-269.

27. *Ibid.,* pp. 270-271.

28. Luther's protector, Frederick the Wise, died in 1525, just after the most serious fighting against the peasants had ended.

CHAPTER NINE

1. This became apparent in the establishment of state churches in Lutheran lands.

2. For an excellent article on the subject see Harold J. Grimm, "Luther, Luther's Critics, and the Peasant Revolt" in Herman Ausubel (ed.), *The Making of Modern Europe*, 2 vols., New York, 1951, I, pp. 108-122. This first appeared as an article in *The Lutheran Church Quarterly*, XIX, 1946, pp. 115-132.

3. Hartmann Grisar, *Luther*. Translation from the German by E. M. Lamond, edited by Luigi Cappadelta, 6 vols., London, 1913-1917, II, p. 193. Even this ardent Catholic scholar recognizes the influence of some of Luther's followers not under the supervision of control of the leader.

4. D. Heinrich Bornkamm, *Luther's World of Thought*, St. Louis, 1958, pp. 12, 14, 19.

5. J. K. F. Knaake and Others (eds.), *D. Martin Luthers Werke, Kritische Gesamtausgabe*, 100 vols., Weimar, 1883-1947, *Briefwechsel*, III, p. 516: "Wohlan, wer den Münzer gesehen hat, der mag sagen, er habe den Teufel leibhaftig gesehen in seinem höchsten Grimm. O Herr Gott, wo solcher Geist in den Bauren auch ist, wie hoche Zeit ist dasz sie erwürget werden wie die tollen Hunde! Denn der Teufel fühlet vielleicht den jungsten Tag, darumb denkt er die Grundsuppe zu rühren und alle hollische Macht auf einmal zu beweisen."

6. Ernst G. Schwiebert, *Luther and His Times. The Reformation from a New Perspective*, p. 546.

7. Albert Hyma, pp. 274, 276.

8. E. L. Enders and G. Kawerau (eds.), *Dr. Martin Luthers Briefwechsel*, 19 vols., Stuttgart, 1893, V, p. 164.

9. J. K. F. Knaake and Others (eds.), *D. Martin Luthers Werke, Kritische Gesamtausgabe*, 100 vols., Weimar, 1883-1947, XVIII, p. 391.

APPENDIX A:

WITTENBERG'S WORTHY ORDINANCE

A. L. Richter (ed.), *Die Evangelischen Kirchenordungen des Sechzehnten Jahrhunderts* (2 vols., Weimar, 1846), II, pp. 484-485.

Anhang.

I.

1522.

Ain löbliche ordnung der Fürstlichen stat Wittemberg Im tausent fünfhundert vnd zwaintzigsten jar auffgericht.

Die von Carlstadt während Luthers Aufenthaltes auf der Wartburg verfaßte, auf 1 B. 4. im Drucke erschiene= ne K.=O. Die Leiſeniger Kaſten=O. ob. Nr. IV. hat aus ihr einzelne Anklänge.

*
* *

Ordnung der Stat Wittemberg Anno domini MDXXII. auffgericht.

Erſtlich iſt einhelligklich beſchloſſen, das all zins der got= helfer, all Prieſterſchafften, vnd alle zins der gewerden, ſollen zuhauffen geſchlagen vnd in ain gemainen kaſten gepracht wer= den, darzu ſeind verordnet zwen des rabts zwen von der gemain, vnd ain ſchreyber, die ſollich zins einnemen, inhaben vnd damit arm leut verſehen ſöllen.

Item es ſöllen hinfüro die zins der lehen der prieſter, wenn die durch abſterben ains prieſters los fallen, auch in den ſelben gemainen kaſten geſchlagen, vnd kainer fürohin verlihen werden.

Es ſol auch kain betler in vnſer ſtat gelitten werden, wellich alters oder kranckhait halben zu arbaiten nit geſchickt ſeind, ſon= der man ſol die zu arbait treiben, oder auß der ſtat verweyſen, die aber auß zufallen als kranckhait oder ander zufall halben von armut wegen, die ſollen auß dem gemainen kaſten durch die ver= ordneten zymlicher weiß verſehen werden 2c.

Item es ſol was ordnuß die ſeind kain terminer bey vns halten.

Item es ſol kainem münch in vnſer ſtat zu betlen geſtattet werden, ſonder ſy mügen ſich ihrer zins die ſy geſund haben, vnd darzu mit iren henden auffhalten vnd neren.

Item es iſt auch inuentiert alles das ſo die kloſter geſund bey vns habent, als kelch, patificalia, monſtrantzen, vnd der glei= chen auch all ir einkommen verzaychnet das ſy beſitzen vnd jär= lich auffzuheben habent.

Item kain frembder ſchuler ſol in vnſer ſtat gelitten werden, wil aber ainer oder mer bey vns ſtudiren der mag ſich ſelb mit eſſen vnd trincken verſehen, dann wir kainem wöllen geſtatten zu betlen noch zu mendicieren.

Item es ſöllen auch die Stationirer noch kainerlay kirchen= bitter nit geduldet werden, in anſehung das alle kirchen beraupt vnd mer dann zuuil gebaut ſeind 2c.

Auß dem gemainen kaſten ſoll man auch armen handtwercks= leuten die on das ir handtwerck nit vermügen täglich zu treyben, leyhen, damit ſy ſich neren mügent, doch daſſelb auff ain geſetzte zeyt wiberumb zugelten, on ainiche verzinſung, welche aber

(continued)

vnuermüglich seind das wider zugeben, den sol man des vmb gots willen erlassen.

Item auß dem gemainen kasten sol man armen wayßen be-sonder junckfrawen zymlicher weyß beraten vnd außgeben auch fünff armer leüt finder.

Item wa aber sollich zinß zu sollichen guten werden nit gnugsam seind, oder sich nitt als weyt erstrecken wurden, so sol man die priester oder burger, nach dem er hat, järlich ain summa gelts, dem armen hauffen zu auffhaltung raychen.

Item die priester die wir yetzund haben, dieweyl it zinß auch in den gemainen kasten gezogen seint, darvon sich yeder järlichen von den Vigilien die sy halten, bey acht guldin järlich versehen werden, dieweyl dann die Meß vnd Vigilien vergeen, mügent sy für das selbig gelt gern krannck leüt ersuchen, vnnd in iren nöten trösten, doch söllen sy nyemant zu Testamentarien bestellen noch halten.

Item die bild vnd altarien in der kirchen söllen auch ab-gethon werden, damit abgötterey zu vermeyden, dann drey altaria on bild genug seind.

Item die messen söllen nit anderst gehalten werden, dann wie sy Christus am abentessen hat eingesetzt, doch vmb ettlicher sachen vmbs glauben willen, lasset man singen, de tempore, vnd nit de sanctis, vnd singet Introitum, Kyrieleison, gloria in excelsis, et in terra, collecta, oder preces, epistel, gradualia, on sequens, evangelium, credo, offertorium, prefatio, Sanctus, on Canonen maior vnd minor, dieweyl die geschrifft nit gemeß seind, darnach bringt an das Evangelisch mal, sein communi-canten, so consecriert der priester, seind sy nit da, so consecriert er vnd summiert es, hat er anders andacht durtzu, darnach con-

cludiert er mit der Collecten, on Ite missa est. Es mag auch der communicant die consecrierten Hostien in die Hand nemen, vnd selbs in den mund schieben, dergleychen auch den kelch, vnd darauß trincken.

Wöllen auch hinfüro nit gestatten, daß vnerlich personen sich füro an bey vns sollen enthalten, sonder söllent zu der ee greyffen, wöllen sy das nit thun, so sy seßhafft seind, sol man sy vertreyben, sein sy aber vnseßhafft, sol in sonderhait der wirt der sy buldet, hochlich gestrafft werden, vnd ober das sollen die, so sy aines vnerlichen wesen oder lebens beschuldigt, auß der stat vertriben werden.

So auch vnser mitburger vnd inwoner mit den zinsen zu hoch beschwert, also, das sy fünff oder sechs guldin vom hundert bißher gegeben, oder mügen Die ablegen, seynd sy des vermü-gens nit, wöllen wir jnen die haubt summa auff dem gemainen kasten thun, also daß sy vier guldin vom hundert dem gemel-nen kasten järlich biß sy die haubt summa ablegen, zinßen. Wir tragen aber zu der Gottlichait bey vns dise zuuersicht, so werden sich hierinnen auch christenlicher liebe beschliessen, vnd sich in dem sonderlichen gutwillig finden lassen.

Auch sol man sonderlich auffsehen haben, so armer leüt finder als finden, die zu der schul vnd studia geschickt seind, vnd doch armut halben darben nit finden bleyben, das man den verleg, damit man alzeit gelert leüt hab, die das haillig Evangelium vnd geschrifft predigen, vnd das auch in weltlichen regimenten, an geschickten leüt nit mangel sey, die aber nitt geschickt seind, sol man jn zu handtwercken oder zu arbayt hal-ten, dann in sollichem sonderlichen auffsehens von nöten ist.

Finis.

APPENDIX B: THE TWELVE ARTICLES

The fundamental and true chief articles of all the peasants and subjects of spiritual and temporal lords, concerning the things in which they feel themselves aggrieved.

To the Christian reader peace, and the grace of God through Christ.

There are many antichristians who have lately taken occasion of the assembling of the peasants to cast scorn upon the Gospel, saying, Is this the fruit of the new Gospel? Is no one to be obedient, but are all to rebel and balk, to run together with force and gather in crowds in order to reform, to overthrow, or perhaps to slay the spiritual and temporal lords? To all these godless and wicked critics the following articles make answer, in order, first, to remove this reproach from the Word of God, and second, to justify in a Christian way the disobedience, nay, the rebellion of the peasants.

First, The Gospel is not a cause of rebellion and disturbance, because it is a message about Christ, the promised Messiah, whose words and life teach nothing but love, peace, patience and unity; and all who believe in this Christ become loving, peaceful, patient and harmonious. This is the foundation of all the articles of the peasants (as will clearly appear), and they are directed to the hearing of the Word of God and to life in accordance with it. How, then, can the antichristians call the Gospel a cause of revolt and disturbance? But the fact that some antichristians and enemies of the Gospel resist these demands and requests is not the fault of the Gospel, but of the devil, the deadliest enemy of the Gospel, who arouses opposition in his own by means of unbelief. Hereby the Word of God, which teaches love, peace, and unity, is suppressed and taken away.

Second, It follows evidently that the peasants, desiring in their articles this Gospel for doctrine and life, cannot be called disobedient and rebellious; but if it be the will of God to hear the peasants, earnestly crying to live according to His Word, who will blame the will of God? Who will meddle in His judgment? Nay, who will resist His majesty? Did He not hear the children of Israel, crying to Him, and release them out of the hand of Pharaoh, and can He not today deliver His own? Yea, He will deliver them, and that quickly! Therefore, Christian reader, read the following articles with care, and afterwards judge.

Here follow the articles.

Adolph Spaeth and Others (eds.), *Works of Martin Luther, with Introduction and Notes* (6 vols., Philadelphia, 1915-1932), IV, pp. 210-216.

THE FIRST ARTICLE

First, It is our humble petition and request, as also the will and intention of all of us, that in the future we should have authority and power so that a whole community should choose and appoint a pastor, and also have the right to depose him, if he should conduct himself improperly. The pastor thus chosen should preach to us the Holy Gospel purely and clearly, without any human addition, doctrine, or commandment; for to proclaim to us continually the true faith gives us cause to pray to God for His grace to instill and confirm this true faith within us, and if His grace is not instilled in us, we always remain flesh and blood, which availeth nothing, since it stands clearly in the Scriptures that only through true faith can we come to God, and only through His mercy can we be saved. Therefore we need a leader and pastor; and thus our demand is grounded on the Scriptures.

THE SECOND ARTICLE

Second, Since the tithe is appointed in the Old Testament and fulfilled in the New, we will none the less gladly pay the just tithe of grain, but in a proper way. Since men ought to give it to God and distribute it to those that are His, it belongs to the pastor who clearly proclaims the Word of God, and we will that, for the future, this tithe be gathered and received by our church-provost, whom a community appoints; that out of it there shall be chosen by an entire community, a modest, sufficient maintenance for him and his, with the consent of the whole community; that the remainder shall be distributed to the poor and needy who are in the same village, according to the circumstances and with the consent of the community. Anything that then remains shall be kept, so that if the needs of the land require the laying of a war-tax, no general tax may be laid upon the poor, but it shall be paid out of this surplus.

If it should happen that there were one or more villages that had sold their tithes to meet certain needs, they are to be informed that he who has the tithes in this way from a whole village is not to be deprived of them without return, but we will come to agreement with him, in proper way, form, and manner, to buy them back from him on suitable terms and at a suitable time. But in case anyone has not bought the tithes from any village, and his forbears have simply appropriated them to themselves, we will not, and ought not, and intend not, to pay him anything further, but will keep them for the support of the aforesaid, our chosen pastor, and for distribution to the needy, as the Holy Scriptures contain, no matter whether the holders of the tithes be spiritual or temporal. The small tithe we will not give at all, for God the Lord created cattle for the free use of men, and we regard this an improper tithe, which men have invented; therefore we will not give it any longer.

THE THIRD ARTICLE

Third, It has been the custom hitherto for men to hold us as their own property; and this is pitiable, seeing that Christ has redeemed and bought us all with the precious shedding of His blood, the lowly as well as the great, excepting no one. Therefore, it agrees with Scripture that we be free and will to be so. Not that we would be entirely free; God does not teach us that we should desire no rulers. We are to live in the commandments, not in the free self-will of the flesh; but we are to love God, recognize Him in our neighbor as our Lord, and do all (as we gladly would do) that God has commanded in the Lord's Supper; therefore, we ought to live according to His commandment. This commandment does not teach us that we are not to be obedient to the rulers, but we are to humble ourselves, not before the rulers only, but before everyone. Thus to our chosen and appointed rulers (appointed for us by God) we are willingly obedient in all proper and Christian matters, and we have no doubt that, as true and real Christians, they will gladly release us from serfdom, or show us in the Gospel that we are serfs.

THE FOURTH ARTICLE

Fourth, It has been the custom hitherto that no poor man has had the power to be allowed to catch game, wild fowl, or fish in running water; and this seems to us altogether improper and unbrotherly, selfish, and not according to the Word of God. In some places the rulers keep the game to spite us and for our great loss, because the unreasoning beasts wantonly devour that property of ours which God causes to grow for the use of man; and we have to endure this and keep quiet about it, though it is against God and neighbor. When God the Lord created man, He gave him authority over all animals, over the birds in the air, and over the fish in the water. Therefore it is our request that if anyone has waters, he offer satisfactory documentary evidence that the waters have been wittingly sold to him; in that case we do not wish to take them from him by force; on the contrary, Christian consideration must be shown, for the sake of brotherly love. But he who cannot bring sufficient proof of this shall surrender them to the community in a proper manner.

THE FIFTH ARTICLE

Fifth, We are also aggrieved in the manner of wood-cutting, for our lords have appropriated all the woods to themselves alone, and when the poor man needs any wood, he must buy it at a double price. It is our opinion that woods held by lords, spiritual or temporal, who have not bought them, should revert to an entire community, and that a community be free, in a regular way, to allow anyone to take home what he needs for firewood without payment, and also to take for nothing any that he needs for wood-working, though with the consent of him whom the community shall choose to supervise this. If there are no woods that have not been thus honestly purchased, a brotherly and Christian agreement should be reached about them; but if the property had first been appropriated and afterwards sold, the agreement shall be made in accordance with the facts in the case, and according to brotherly love and the Holy Scriptures.

THE SIXTH ARTICLE

Sixth, We have a heavy grievance because of the services which are increased from day to day, and grow daily. We desire that this matter be properly looked into and that we be not so heavily burdened, but that gracious regard be had to us, as our ancestors rendered services only according to the Word of God.

THE SEVENTH ARTICLE

Seventh, We will not henceforth allow ourselves to be further oppressed by the lords, but a man shall possess his holding in accordance with the terms on which it has been granted, according to the agreement between lord and peasant. The lord shall not compel him further, or force him to more services, or demand anything else from him for nothing, so that the peasant may use and enjoy his holding unburdened and peacefully; but if the lord needs more services, the peasant shall be willing and obedient, though at such times as may not work the peasant injury, and he shall perform the services for proper pay.

THE EIGHTH ARTICLE

Eighth, We are greatly aggrieved, as many of us have holdings, because the said holdings will not support the rents, and the peasants suffer loss and ruin. (We ask) that the lords have honorable men inspect the said holdings, and fix a fair rent, so that the peasant shall not labor for nothing, for every laborer is worthy of his hire.

THE NINTH ARTICLE

Ninth, We are aggrieved by the great wrong of continually making new laws. Punishment is inflicted on us, not according to the facts in the case, but at times by great ill-will, at times by great favor. In our opinion we should be punished by the ancient written law, and the cases dealt with according to the facts, and not according to favor.

THE TENTH ARTICLE

Tenth, We are aggrieved because some have appropriated to themselves meadows out of the common fields, which once belonged to a community. We would take these back again into the hands of our communities, unless they have been honestly purchased; but if they have been unjustly purchased, we should come to a kindly and brotherly agreement about them, according to the facts in the case.

THE ELEVENTH ARTICLE

Eleventh, We would have the custom called Todfall entirely abolished. We will not suffer it, or allow widows and orphans to be so shamefully robbed, against God and honor, as now happens in many places, under many forms, and that by those who ought to guard and protect them. They have skinned and scraped us, and though they had little authority, they have taken that. God will no longer suffer it; it shall be entirely done away; no man shall henceforth be bound to give anything of it, whether little or much.

CONCLUSION

Twelfth, It is our conclusion and final opinion that, if one or more of the articles here set forth were not to be in agreement with the Word of God (though we think this is not the case), these articles, when they are shown to us by the Word of God to be improper, we will recede from, if this is explained to us with arguments of Scripture. If some of the articles were conceded to us, and it were afterwards found that they were unjust, they shall be from that hour null and void, and have no more force; likewise, if in the Scriptures, with the truth, more things were discovered that were against God and injurious to our neighbors, we will, and we have determined to, use forbearance and practice and exercise ourselves in all Christian doctrine. Therefore we will pray to God the Lord, for He, and none other can give us this. The peace of Christ be with us all.

SELECT BIBLIOGRAPHY

The following bibliography does not pretend to be complete nor does it pretend to be an exhaustive list of the more important works of Luther. It is as the title indicates a select bibliography. Selection was based on the following criteria: 1) titles cited in the manuscript are listed; 2) those works which I have found very useful but which I have not necessarily cited; and 3) those works which I consider might be useful to the reader to obtain more information on specific topics.

The serious scholar will undoubtedly find omissions in the list. He might also be critical of the form of the bibliography, preferring perhaps the annotated list or the bibliographical note. It is my hope that the select bibliography will be of use to those who feel a need for it and who want to use it.

Bibliographical guides are of tremendous aid to the Luther student. Roland H. Bainton's *Bibliography of the Continental Reformation: Materials Available in English* (Chicago: American Society of Church History, 1935), even though outdated by the rush of recent publication, is still a good guide to the material in English. Dahlmann-Waitz's *Quellenkunde der Deutschen Geschichte* (Leipzig: Koehler, 1912), is a standard bibliography of German history which has to be consulted. The outstanding bibliography, however, continues to be Karl Schottenloher's *Bibliographie zur deutschen Geschichte im Zeitalter der Glaubensspaltung 1517-1585 im Auftrag der Kommission zur Erforschung der Reformation und Gegenreformation* (Leipzig: Hiersemann, 1938, 7 vols.).

No study however can be static, and it is necessary to keep a watchful eye out for new titles from the publishers, and to pursue contantly the bibliographies in the scholarly works of others. Such examination invariably turns up new material which has to be examined. For instance the articles in the *Twentieth Century Encyclopedia of Religious Knowledge: An Extension of the New Schaff Herzog Encyclopedia of Religious Knowledge* is invaluable for the articles on the Peasants' War and related persons and events.

No study can be carried out without actually working with the collected works of Martin Luther. The student of the Reformation and particularly the student of the Reformer is indeed fortunate to have such a large number of these collections. Below are listed these collections which form the basis of this study.

D. Martin Luthers Werke, Kritische Gesamtausgabe edited by J. K. F. Knaake and Others (Weimar: Herman Böhlau, 1883-1947, 100 vols.). This collection is divided into sections or collections of his letters and correspondence, the German Bible, the Table Talks, and the majority of the volumes to his tracts, sermons, commentaries, and so forth. It remains the outstanding collection, but it still must be used with care. *Dr. Martin Luthers Sämmtliche Werke* (Erlangen: Heyder, 1826-1854, 67 vols.) is the older but still useful collection.

In 1955 the announcement was made that an American Edition was to be published. Originally it was to consist of 55 volumes. It has been expanded to 56 volumes and a large number have already been published although the set is still incomplete. Jaroslav Pelikan and Helmut Lehmann are the general editors. *Luther's Works* (St. Louis and Philadelphia, 1955, 56 vols.). Several other English editions have appeared, and I have used the Philadelphia (Holman) Edition to check my own translations from the Weimar. Originally intended to be a selection comprising ten volumes, only six have been published and since the collection began appearing in 1915 it seems that the number is fixed at six. This is the *Works of Martin Luther, with Introduction and Notes* edited by Adolph Spaeth and Others (Philadelphia: Lutheran Pub., 1915-1932, 6 vols.).

All of the translations which appear have been taken from either the Philadelphia Edition or from the new American Edition. It is significant that the editors and translators of the newer edition have changed very little the work of those remarkable scholars who participated in that venture which led to the Philadelphia Edition. This is a compliment and also praise of the earlier work. Since I am not an expert in the German language, my own translation from the Weimar Edition would have been greatly inferior to that of the Philadelphia group. It would have been presumptious to have included my own poor work. I have used the Weimar Edition as was indicated above. And I have compared my translation with that of others. The others, however, have taken precedence over my own concerning its appearance in this present study.

In addition to the collection of letters and correspondence in the Weimar edition, a number of other collections have also been used: *Dr. Martin Luthers Briefwechsel,* edited by E. L. Enders and G. Kawerau (Leipzig: Rudolf Haupt, 1884-1920, 19 vols.); Margaret A. Currie's *The Letters of Martin Luther* (London: Macmillan, 1908); and Preserved Smith's *Life and*

Letters of Martin Luther (Boston: Houghton, 1912). This last collection has been updated and expanded in Preserved Smith and Charles M. Jacob's *Luther's Correspondence and Other Contemporary Letters* (Philadelphia: Lutheran Pub., 1913-1918, 2 vols.).

The following list, grouped alphabetically, consists of biographies, specific monographic studies on the Peasants' War, and special studies concerning Luther's economic and political theories.

Althaus, Paul. *Luthers Haltung im Bauernkrieg*. Basel: Benno Schwabe, 1953.

Bainton, Roland H. *Here I Stand. A Life of Martin Luther*. Nashville and New York: Abingdon-Cokesbury, 1950.

Barge, Hermann. *Andreas Bodenstein von Karlstadt*. Leipzig: 1905, 2 vols.

Bax, Ernest Belfort. *The Peasants' War in Germany 1525-1526*. London: Swan Sonnenschein, 1899.

Beard, Charles A. *Martin Luther and the Reformation in Germany Until the Close of the Diet of Worms*. London: Green, 1896.

Bender, Harold S. "Anabaptists" in *Twentieth Century Encyclopedia of Religious Knowledge: An Extension of the New Schaff Herzog Encyclopedia of Religious Knowledge*. Grand Rapids, Michigan: Baker, 1955, 2 vols.

Berbig, Dr. Georg. *Spalatin und sein Verhältnis zu Martin Luther auf Grund ihres Briefwechsels biz zum Jahre 1525*. Halle: Curt Nietschamplotz'-sche Buchdruckerei Verlagsbuchhandlung, 1906.

Bloch, Ernst. *Thomas Münzer Als Theologe Der Revolution*. Berlin, Augbau-Verlag, 1921, 1960.

Böhmer, Heinrich. *Der junge Luther*. Gotha: Flamberg, 1925.

_____. *Luther and the Reformation in the Light of Modern Research*. New York: MacVeagh, 1930. Translated by E. S. G. Potter.

Bornkamm, D. Heinrich. "Carlstadt" in *Twentieth Century Encyclopedia of Religious Knowledge: An Extension of the New Schaff Herzog Encyclopedia of Religious Knowledge*. Grand Rapids, Michigan: Baker, 1955, 2 vols.

_____. *Luther's World of Thought*. St. Louis: Concordia, 1958. Translated by Martin A. Bertram.

Brinton, Crane. *The Making of the Modern Mind*. New York: Mentor Book, 1956.

Clemen, Otto (ed.). *Luthers Werke in Auswahl, Unter Mitwirkung von Albert Leitsmann*. Bonn: 1912-1913, 4 vols.

Dickens, A. G. *Reformation and Society in Sixteenth-Century Europe*. New York: Harcourt, Brace and World, 1966.

Dillenberger, John. "Survey Literature in Luther Studies 1950-1955." Ch. Hist. Vol. XXV, No. 1, June, 1955, pp. 160-177.

_____. "Major Volumes and Selected Periodical Literature in Luther

Studies, 1956-1959." Ch. Hist. XXX, No. 1, March, 1961, pp. 61-87.

Fast, Heinold. (ed.) (Comp.) *Der Linke Fluegel Der Reformation.* Glaubens-Zeugnisse Der Taufer. Spiritualisten, Schwarmer, Und Antitrinitarier. (Klassiker Des Protestantismus IV, Sammlung Dietrich, BD. 269).

Fichter, Heinrich. *Ulrich Von Hutten: Ein Leben Für Die Freiheit.* Pahl: Hohewarte, 1954.

Fife, Robert Herndon. *The Revolt of Martin Luther.* New York: Columbia University Press, 1957.

Forell, George Wolfgang. *Faith Active in Love: An Investigation of the Principles Underlying Luther's Social Ethics.* New York: American Press, 1954.

_____. *Thomas Münzer: Symbol and Reality.* Dialog, 1963, pp. 12-23.

Franz, Günther. *Der deutsche Bauernkrieg.* Munich and Berlin: Oldenburg, 1933, 2 vols. Second ed., 1956.

Friedenburg, Walter (ed.). *Urkundenbuch der Universitaet Wittenberg.* Magdeburg: 1926-27, 2 vols.

Friedmann, Robert. "Thomas Muentzer's Relation to Anabaptism." *The Mennonite Quarterly Review.* Vol. XXXI. April, 1957, No. 2, pp. 75-87.

Friesen, Abraham. "Thomas Müntzer in Marxist Thought." *Church Hist.,* Sept., 1965, Vol. XXXIV, No. 3, pp. 306-327.

Gerdes, Hayo. *Luthers Streit mit den Schwarmern um das rechte Verständnis des Gesetzes Mose.* Gottingen: Verlaganstalt, 1955.

Greshat, M. "Luther's Haltung Im Bauernkrieg." In *Archiv Für Reformationsgeschichte.* Jahrgang 56, 1965. Heft. 1, pp. 31-47.

Grimm, Harold J. "Luther, Luther's Critics, and the Peasant Revolt." *Making of Modern Europe.* Vol. I, edited by Herman Ausubel. New York: Dryden, 1951.

_____. "Peasants' War" in *Twentieth Century Encyclopedia of Religious Knowledge: An Extension of the New Schaff Herzog Encyclopedia of Religious Knowledge.* Grand Rapids, Michigan: Baker, 1955, 2 vols.

_____. *The Reformation Era.* New York: Macmillan, 1954.

_____. "Social Forces in the German Reformation." *Church Hist.* March, 1962, Vol. XXXI, No. 1, pp. 3-13.

Grimm, Heinrich. *Ulrich von Hutten und seine Drucker.* Wiesbaden: Otto Harrassowitz, 1956.

Grisar, Hartmann. *Luther.* London: Trubner; St. Louis: Herder, 1913, 6 vols. Translated by E. M. Lamond.

Gritsch, Eric W. *Reformer Without a Church. The Life and Thought of Thomas Muentzer.* Philadelphia: Fortress Press, 1967.

_____. "Thomas Muentzer and the Origins of Protestant Spiritualism." *Mennonite Quarterly Review.* Vol. XXXVII, No. 3, July, 1963, pp. 172-194.

Hartfelder, Karl. *Geschichte des Bauernkrieges in Sudwestdeutschland.*

Stuttgart: J. G. Getta'schen Buchhandlung, 1884.

Hillerbrand, Hans J. *A Fellowship of Discontent.* New York: Harper and Row, 1967.

————. *A Bibliography of Anabaptism,* 1520-1630. Elkhart, Indiana: Inst. of Mennonite Studies, 1962.

————. "The Origin of Sixteenth Century Anabaptism: Another Look." *Archiv Fur Reformations—Geschichte,* LII (1962, 152-180).

————. "Anabaptism and the Reformation: Another Look." *Ch. Hist.,* Vol. XXIX, No. 4., December, 1960, pp. 404-423.

————. "Andreas Bodenstein of Carlstadt, Prodigal Reformer." *Ch. Hist.,* Vol. XXXXV, No. 4, December, 1966, pp. 379-398.

————. "Thomas Muntzer's Last Tract Against Mratin Luther." *MQR,* Vol. XXXVIII. January, 1964, Number One, pp. 20-36.

Hinrichs, Carl. *Luther Und Muntzer Ihre Auseinandersetzung Uber Obrigkeit Und Widerstandrecht.* Berlin, W. De Gruyter, 1952.

Hitchcock, William R. *The Background of the Knights' Revolt, 1522-23.* Berkeley and Los Angeles: Univ. of California Publications in History, Vol. 61, 1958.

Holborn, Hajo. *Ulrich von Hutten.* Leipzig, 1929. English translation by Roland H. Bainton. *Ulrich von Hutten and the German Reformation.* New Haven: Yale University Press, 1937.

————. *A History of Modern German: The Reformation.* New York: Knopf. 1959.

Hutten, Ulrich von. *Equitis Germani Opera,* edited by Edward Boecking. Leipzig: 1859, 7 vols.

Hyma, Albert. "Charles V, Emperor" in *Twentieth Century Encyclopedia of Religious Knowledge: An Extension of the New Schaff Herzog Encyclopedia of Religious Knowledge.* Grand Rapids, Michigan: Baker, 1955, 2 vols.

————. *Christianity and Politics. A History of the Principles and Struggles of Church and State.* Philadelphia: Lippincott, 1938.

————. *Christianity, Capitalism, and Communism.* Ann Arbor: Wahr, 1937.

————. "Erasmus and the Sacrament of Matrimony" in *Archiv für Reformationsgeschichte.* Vol. XLVIII, 1957.

————. "Holy Roman Empire" in *Twentieth Century Encyclopedia of Religious Knowledge: An Extension of the New Schaff Herzog Encyclopedia of Religious Knowledge.* Grand Rapids, Michigan: Baker, 1955, 2 vols.

————. "Investiture" in *Twentieth Century Encyclopedia of Religious Knowledge: An Extension of the New Schaff Herzog Encyclopedia of Religious Knowledge.* Grand Rapids, Michigan: Baker, 1955, 2 vols.

————. *Luther's Theological Development from Erfurt to Augsburg.* New York: Crofts, 1928.

_____. *New Light on Martin Luther*. Grand Rapids, Michigan: Eerdmans, 1958.

_____. *Renaissance to Reformation*. Grand Rapids, Michigan: Eerdmans, Rev. ed., 1955.

Kamnitzer, Heinz. *Zur Vorgeschichte des deutschen Bauernkrieges*. Berlin: Rütten und Loenig, 1953.

Kiessling, Elmer Carl. *The Early Sermons of Luther and their Relation to the Pre-Reformation Sermon*. Grand Rapids, Michigan: Zondervan, 1940.

Klaehn, Karsten. *Luthers Sozialethische Haltung im Bauernkrieg*. Rostock: Carl Hinstorffs Buchdruckerei, 1940.

Kupisch, Karl. *Feinde Luthers: Vier Historische Bildnisse*, Berlin: Lettner-Verlag, 1951.

Lauppe, E. "Schwarzacher Haufen" in *Ortenau*, Vol. XXXIV, 1954.

Lilje, Hans. *Luther Now*. Philadelphia: Muhlenberg, 1952.

Lindsay, Thomas M. *A History of the Reformation*. New York: Scribner, 1910, 2 vols.

McGiffert, Arthur C. *Martin Luther. The Man and His Work*. New York: Century, 1910.

McGovern, Wm. M. *From Luther to Hitler: The History of Fascist-Nazi Political Philosophy*. Boston: Houghton-Mifflin, 1941.

MacKinnon, James. *Luther and the Reformation*. New York and London: Longmans, 1925, 4 vols.

Manschreck, Clyde Leonard. *Melanchthon: The Quiet Reformer*. Nashville: Abingdon, 1958.

Maritain, Jacques. *Three Reformers*. London: Sheed and Ward, 1928.

Meissinger, Karl August. *Luther, Die deutsche Tragödie, 1521*. Bern: Francke Verlag, 1953.

_____. *Der Katolische Luther*. München: Leo Lehnen Verlag, 1952.

Melanchthon, Philip. *Opera* in *Corpus Reformatorum*, edited by Karl Bretschneider and Heinrich Bindseil. Halle: 1834-1909, 97 vols.

Meusel, A. *Thomas Müntzer und seine Zeit*. Berlin: H. Kamnitzer, 1952.

Münzer, Thomas. *Politsche Schriften, Mit Kommentar Hrsw*. Von Carl Hinrichs Halle (Salle) M. Niemeyer, 1959.

_____. *Schriften Und Briefe Kritische Gesamtausgabe Unter Mitarbeit*. Von Paul Kirn Herausgegeben Von Gunther Franz. Gutersloh, 1968.

Nanta, D. and Hyma, Albert. "Thomas Muenzer" in *Twentieth Century Encyclopedia of Religious Knowledge: An Extension of the New Schaff Herzog Encyclopedia of Religious Knowledge*. Grand Rapids, Michigan: Baker, 1955, 2 vols.

Napperdey, Thomas. "Theologie Und Revolution Bei Thomas Müntzer" in *Archiv Für Reformationsgeschichte*. Jahrgang 54 . . . 1963, Heft 2, pp. 145-181.

Olsson, Herbert. *Grundproblemet i Luthers Socialtik.* Lund: Linstedts Univ. Bokhandel, 1934.

Oyer, John S. *Lutheran Reformers Against Anabaptists: Luther, Melanchthon and Menius and the Anabaptists of Central Europe.* The Hague: M. Nifhoff, 1964.

Pascal, Roy. *Social Basis of the German Reformation.* London: Watts, 1933.

Pianzola, Maurice. *Thomas Münzer: Ou, La Guerre De Paysans,* Paris, Club Francais Du Livre, 1958.

Pietsch, Friedrich. "Die Artikel der Limpurger Bauern" in *Zeitschrift für Württembergische Landesgeschichte.* Vol. XIII, 1954.

Plass, Ewald M. *This is Luther.* St. Louis: Concordia, 1948.

_____. *What Luther Says.* St. Louis: Concordia, 1959, 3 vols.

Polack, W. G. *Martin Luther in English Poetry.* St. Louis: Concordia, 1938.

Preuss, Hans. *Martin Luther der Künstler.* Gütersloh: Bertelsmann, 1931.

Reu, Michael. *Luther and the Scriptures.* Columbus: Wartburg, 1944.

_____. *Luther's German Bible: An Historical Presentation together with a Collection of Sources.* Columbus: Lutheran Book, 1934.

Richter, A. L. ed. *Die Evangelischen Kirchenordungen des Sechzehnten Jahrhunderts.* Weimar, 1846, 2 vols.

Ritter, G. "Lutheranism, Catholicism, and the Humanistic View of Life." in *Archiv für Reformationsgeschichte.* Vol. XL, 1953.

Robbert, George S. "A Checklist of Luther's Writings in English." *Concordia Theological Monthly,* 1965, 36:772-792.

Rupp, E. Gordon. *The Righteousness of God, Luther Studies.* London: Hodder and Stoughton, 1953.

Schaefer, Dr. Heinrich. *Pfarrkirche und Stift im deutschen Mittelalter Eine Kirchenrechtsgeschichtliche Untersuchung.* Stuttgart: Verlag Von Ferdinand Enke, 1903.

Schapiro, Jacob S. "Social Reform and the Reformation" in *Studies in History, Economics, and Public Law,* edited by the faculty of Political Science of Columbia University. New York: Columbia Univ. Press, 1909, Vol. XXXIV.

Scheel, Otto, ed. *Dokumente zu Luthers Entwicklung.* Tübingen: Mohr, 1911.

_____. *Martin Luther vom Katholizismuszur Reformation.* Tübingen: Mohr, 1921.

Schwiebert, Ernst G. *Luther and His Times. The Reformation from a New Perspective.* St. Louis: Concordia, 1950.

_____. *Reformation Lectures Delivered at Valparaiso University.* Valparaiso: Schwiebert, 1937.

_____. "Review of Robert Herndon Fife's *The Revolt of Martin Luther.*" *Renaissance News,* Vol. XI, Autumn, 1958, No. 3.

Seebohm, Frederic. *The Era of the Protestant Reformation.* New York: Scribner, 1895.

Smirin, M. M. *Die Volksreformation des Thomas Münzer und der grosze Bauernkrieg*. Berlin, 1952.

Smith, Preserved. *The Age of the Reformation*. New York: Holt, 1920.

Stayer, James M. "Terrorism, The Peasants' War, and the 'Wiedertaufer' " in *Archiv Für Reformations Geschichte* Jahrgang 56 . . . 1965, Heft 2, pp. 227-229.

Strand, Kenneth A., ed. *The Dawn of Modern Civilization: Studies in Renaissance, Reformation and Other Topics Presented to Honor Albert Hyma*. Ann Arbor: Ann Arbor Publishers, 1962.

Suchenwirth, Richard. *Deutsche Geschichte*. Leipzig: Georg Dollheimer, 1934.

Tulloch, John. *Luther and other Leaders of the Reformation*. Edinburgh and London: Blackwood, 1883.

Verduin, Leonard. Articles written for the September, 1958, issues of *The Banner*.

Waas, Adolf. "Ulrich Schmidt von Sulmingen" in *Ulm und Oberschwaben*. Vol. XXXIII, 1953.

_____. *Die Bauern Im Kampf Um Gerechtigkeit 1300-1525*. München: Verlag Georg D. W. Callwey, 1964.

Wace, Henry. *Principles of the Reformation, Practical and Historical*. New York: American Tract Society, n.d.

Walder, Ernst. "Politischen Gehalt der 12 Artikel der deutschen Bauernschaft von 1525." *Schweizer Beiträge zur Allgemeinen Geschichte*. Vol. XII, 1954.

Wappler, Paul. *Thomas Müntzer Im Zwickau Und Die Zwickauer Propheten*. Zwickau: R. Zuckler, 1908.

Waring, Luther Hess. *Political Theories of Martin Luther*. New York and London: Putnam, 1910.

Weigand, Hermann T. "A Close-up of the German Peasants' War." *Transactions of the Conn. Academy of Arts and Sciences*. New Haven: 1944, Vol. XXXV.

Wiechert, Ernst. *Zwei Novelle* edited by Siegfried B. Puknat. New York: Dryden, 1952.

Williams, George Huntston. *The Radical Reformation*. Philadelphia: Westminster Press, 1962.

Zimmermann, Willhelm. *Allgemeine Geschichte Des Grossen Bauernkriegs 3 Bde 1841-1843* (Das Um Frassendste Werk, Aber Vielfach Legends) Stuttgart, 1841-1843. Neuegan Z Ungeabeitete Auflage In Zwei Banden, Stuttgart, 1856.

INDEX

Agricola, 55
Albert, Count of Mansfeld, 55
Althaus, Paul, 145 n.1
Amsdorf, Nicholas, 1, 59, 92
Arme Conrad, 35, 50, 109

Black Troop, the, 46, 50
Bora, Katherine von (Katie), 60, 71, 72, 77, 121, 122, 128, 132, 133
Borna, 8, 122, 126
Bornkamm, Professor D. Heinrich, 132, 141 n.2
Bundschuh, the, 31, 35, 52, 109

Carlstadt. *See* Karlstadt
Charles V, Holy Roman Emperor, 1, 15, 18, 21, 36, 78, 79, 118

Drechsel, Thomas, 5

Ebernburg, 20, 21, 139 n.6
Eisenach, 66, 69
Eisleben, 55, 57, 67, 69, 122, 125, 135
Engels, Friedrich, 63
Erasmus, 18, 20, 21, 30, 129
Erfurt, University of, 69

Frankenhausen, Battle of, 40, 44, 46, 58, 59, 129, 130, 134
Frederick the Wise, Elector of Saxony, 2, 8, 21, 57, 64, 70, 78, 127, 138 n.23
Free Knight of the Empire, 15, 18, 19
Fuggers, the, 27, 69, 90, 121, 133

Gaismair, Michael, 43, 46-50, 109

Geyer, Florian, 43, 45, 46, 49, 50

Hutten, Ulrich von, 14, 16-18, 20-22, 138 n.2
Hyma, Professor Albert, 72, 141 n.2, 142 n.1

Junker, Georg, 2, 4, 8

Kamnitzer, Heinz, 62, 64, 142 n.1
Karlstadt, 2-4, 6-9, 11, 37, 39, 43-45, 47, 64, 109, 123-24, 132, 134, 137 n.4, 140 n.7

Landstuhl, 20
Link, Wenceslaus, 8
Lupfen, Count of, 33
Luther, Hans, 65-69, 133
Luther, Margarethe, 67-68

Magdeburg, 69
Mansfeld, 53-56, 59, 67-69, 77, 135
Melanchthon, Philip, 2, 5, 55, 65, 123
Memmingen, 41, 49, 51
Meusel, Alfred, 64
Moehra, 66, 69
Müller, Hans, 34
Münzer, Thomas, 35, 43, 44, 49-51, 59, 62-64, 94, 109, 110, 113, 127, 130, 132, 134, 140 n.6

Nordhausen, 56, 57, 135

Philip of Hesse, 19, 23

Richard of Greiffenklau, Elector and Archbishop of Trier, 19
Rohrbach, Jäcklein, 50, 130

163